Classic Basket Quilts

Classic Basket Quilts

by
Liz Porter & Marianne Fons

"No quilt collection of our grandmother's day was complete without a basket quilt."
– **Carrie A. Hall, 1935**

American Quilter's Society

P. O. Box 3290 • Paducah, KY 42002-3290

Published by the
American Quilter's Society.
P.O. Box 3290, Paducah, KY 42002-3290

**Library of Congress
Cataloging-in-Publication Data**

Porter, Liz
CLASSIC BASKET QUILTS/by Liz Porter and Marianne Fons.
p. cm.
ISBN: 0-89145-973-1: $16.95
(1. Patchwork–Patterns. 2. Quilting–Patterns.) I. Fons, Marianne.
II. Title.
TT835.P655 1991 746. 46–dc20 91-6664

Additional copies of this book may be ordered from: American Quilter's Society
P.O. Box 3290, Paducah, KY 42002-3290 @ $16.95. Add $1.00 for postage & handling.

Printed by IMAGE GRAPHICS, INC., Paducah, Kentucky

This book is dedicated to the Winterset Public Library, Winterset, Iowa – and to all public libraries, for their wealth of resources and quiet corners.

ACKNOWLEDGMENTS

Photography by Perry Struse, Rural American Graphics, Des Moines, Iowa, except Baskets and Bows Quilt, page 70, Baskets, Big and Little, pages 112 & 115, and Red Flower Basket, page 126. The photography was done at Living History Farms in Des Moines, Iowa, at the Madison County Historical Complex, Winterset, Iowa, and at the home of Dale and Esther Frank, Winterset, Iowa.

The authors would like to thank the people listed below for work on projects in the book. They also wish to thank Katie Porter and Rebecca Fons for modeling and Living History Farms interpreters Josie Jacques and Jan Libby for holding quilts. All projects not mentioned below were made by Liz Porter and Marianne Fons.

Joyce Aufderheide, Nine-Block Sampler .... page 99
Donna Brayman, Tiny Baskets Bed Quilt .... page 65
Marian Brockschmidt, Baskets, Big and Little .... pages 112 & 115
Cathy Bruett, Twelve-Basket Quilt with Pieced Border .... page 76
Ann Chase, Nine-Basket Wall Quilt .... page 29
Barb Corsbie, quilting, Cactus Basket Wall Quilt .... page 81
Dorothy Crowdes, Garden Maze Baby Quilt .... page 100
Maxine Engstrom, Bowl of Flowers .... page 123
Candace Head, Cake Stand Wall Quilt .... page 48
Barb Hendricks, Sawtooth Border Wall Quilt .... page 61
Jeanne Kuentzel, Parquet Basket Bed Quilt .... page 64
Helen Martens, quilting, Triple Irish Chain Quilt .... page 22
  Baskets & Bows Quilt .... page 70
  Scrap Flowerpot Bed Quilt .... page 45
Doris Porter, quilting, One-Basket Wall Quilt .... page 81
Katie Porter, Crumb Basket Wall Quilt .... page 30
Theresa Westrup, Nine-Block Sampler Wall Quilt .... page 99
Bev Young, Twenty-Four-Block Sampler with Pieced Border .... page 94
Darlene Zimmerman, Mini-Baskets Wall Quilt .... page 67
  Nine-Block Sampler Wall Quilt .... page 99

CONTENTS

INTRODUCTION

Classic Basket Quilts is a combination of projects from our successful 1984 book *Classic Basket Patterns* and new projects designed and made since the release of that publication. Many of you may own a much-used copy of that now out-of-print quilt book. We are indebted to the American Quilter's Society for making this revised and expanded collection of traditional basket patterns and projects available to quilters everywhere.

Basket patterns date from the eighteenth century and are still among the best-loved designs for quilts. Their variety, versatility and charm give them special appeal for the quilter. Whether used individually in a small project, or in quantity for a quilt, baskets perfectly exemplify the tradition of patchwork and appliqué designs inspired by everyday household objects.

Our purpose with this book is to bring together a number of basket styles and treatments in a highly usable form, so that you, the quilter, can combine patterns, ideas and settings as you please. The book includes fully-drafted patterns for dozens of patchwork and appliqué basket blocks. Most of the blocks are given in both 6" and 12" sizes. We present projects, with full instructions and yardage requirements, for using baskets in a variety of ways. As you survey the projects, keep in mind that, in every case, different blocks can be substituted in the projects. Yardages are given for each project as shown and are based on 44/45" wide fabric.

You'll also find in *Classic Basket Quilts* a section of general instructions that includes special basket handle ideas, some speed cutting and piecing techniques, tips on appliqué, mitering borders, binding quilts and making hanging loops and sleeves. Since basket blocks are so often set diagonally, we have included a detailed section on the diagonal set, with charts and instructions which can be applied to any diagonally-set project.

Highlights of the appliqué baskets section of the book are baskets made by appliquéing woven fabric strips. The technique we have developed for these unusual baskets was inspired by baskets on the famed Baltimore Album quilts of the mid-nineteenth century.

Finally, we have included several lovely, full-size quilting designs to be used with the given projects and added to your collection.

Whether you choose to create a wallhanging, a special album cover or pillow for a quick-to-complete gift, or to create a full-size bed quilt, we hope you will enjoy working with basket designs as much as we do. We hope, also, that you find our book a useful, inspiring addition to your quiltmaker's library.

Sincerely,

Liz and Marianne

GENERAL INSTRUCTIONS

ABOUT THE PATTERNS

PATCHWORK PATTERNS: The patchwork patterns in this book are organized according to their structure: four-patch, five-patch, six-patch, upright, seven-patch and diamond baskets. Full-size patterns are given for both 12" and 6" finished block sizes. 6" template patterns for blocks appear first in each section and are labeled with lower case letters. The 12" block patterns are labeled with upper case letters. Piecing diagrams are included on the pattern pages.

Note that *all pattern pieces are drawn to finished size*. Seam allowances (¼") must be added. In some cases, where background squares are needed or if the pattern pieces are relatively large, small diagrams will indicate the template size. For example, a diagram like the one shown (Figure 1) may call for a right-angle triangle with 9" legs. *Don't forget to add ¼" seam allowances to these pieces, too.* Note, also, that suggested grain lines are indicated on the pattern pieces.

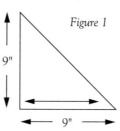

Figure 1

Many of the patchwork baskets have appliquéd handles or contents. Handles are made of curved bias strips. See headings below for instructions on using the handle placement guides and making curved handles from bias.

APPLIQUÉ PATTERNS: The appliqué patterns in this book vary in size. The Eyelet Nosegay, French Basket and Plaid Basket can be made as 12" blocks as well as used in the projects as illustrated. For most appliqué patterns, you can vary the size of your project easily by changing the size of the background fabric.

Note that *all pattern pieces are drawn to finished size*. Seam allowances (¼") must be added. Curved basket handles are made from folded bias strips. See section on handles (page 11).

A WORD ABOUT METRICS

This book gives measurements for U.S. standards only. To find the metric equivalent, multiply inches by 2.54 to convert them to centimeters. A yard is equivalent to .914 meters.

MAKING AND USING TEMPLATES

For making templates, we recommend a thin plastic that can be cut with scissors. Many quilting and craft stores stock sheets of a translucent material designed especially for making templates. The cut edges don't wear down with repeated use and the translucence helps when we want to position a stripe or print in a certain way. Also, template shapes are easily traced from the book to this see-through material.

We make our templates finished size and then add the seam allowance markings on the fabric. For patchwork, draw around the template on the *wrong* side of the fabric, then measure a ¼" seam allowance with a transparent ruler and mark the cutting line. The inner line is the sewing line. To mark for appliqué, use a removable marker and draw around the template on the *right* side of the cloth. Cut approximately ¼" to the outside of this turn-under line.

Some people prefer to make templates that already include a seam allowance so they can mark only the cutting line on the fabric. Use the method that works best for you.

TIPS ON PATCHWORK

Patchwork can be sewn by hand or by machine. If you sew by hand, you can begin and end your stitching on seam lines; your seam allowances are then "free" and you can press them as you wish to prevent their showing through lighter pieces. You can also press seam thicknesses away from planned quilting lines.

We generally sew our patchwork by machine. It's quicker, of course, and we feel the stitching is stronger. Also, "chaining" and assembly-line techniques can be employed for speed. (See the *Quick Piecing Techniques* section on page 13.) With machine-sewn patchwork, however, seam allowances are sewn down when seams are crossed by others. As you construct and add units to the block, give some thought to these seams. Before you stitch, press seam allowances so that dark fabric seams will not detract from your work by showing through lighter fabrics. In some cases, however, you will find that seams must be allowed to go the way they want to for the patchwork to lie flat.

Patchwork triangles are generally cut so that only one side of the fabric is on the bias (Figure 2). A bias edge is apt to stretch out of shape with handling, and a few stretched pieces will ruin your block. With basket blocks, the bias sides of triangles often occur across the

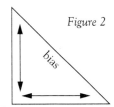

Figure 2

top edge of the basket, an edge that is joined to the bias edge of one large triangle, i.e., the upper, or handle, section of the block. Be extra careful when sewing these seams. Before joining the two sections, pin the corners, matching sewing lines. Pin gently along the seam (Figure 3). You can correct a certain amount of discrepancy in seam length, whether you

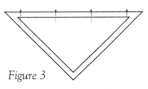

Figure 3

are piecing by hand or by machine. By hand, you can take up, or "ease in" any extra fullness gradually as you sew the seam. If you machine piece, place the longer side (the side that needs taking up) on the bottom as you put it through the machine. The feed dogs of the sewing machine will take up extra fullness as the cloth goes through.

Another point to remember about triangles is that when the long side (the hypotenuse) of a triangle occurs on the outside edge of a patchwork block or a diagonal set quilt, you should cut that edge on the straight of the grain (Figure 4). If those edges are bias, they will stretch and may cause "ruffled" edges.

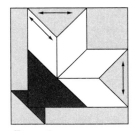

Figure 4

Bias is also a factor with diamonds. Cut diamonds so that two parallel edges are on straight grain (unless you want to position a stripe point to point).

TIPS ON APPLIQUÉ

FABRIC: Appliqué experts recommend 100% cotton fabric for appliqué. When finger-pressed or pinched, cotton will "stay put," while blends "spring back." Also, cotton frays less, so small cut pieces hold up better.

PREPARATION: To prepare fabric pieces for appliqué, fold the seam allowance back along the drawn fold line and baste, keeping the basting close to the fold. Another method is to forego the basting and turn the seam allowance back with the needle as you appliqué. We generally baste, but like to use the tip of the needle, while appliquéing, to slip under the appliqué piece to smooth out any "bumps." Remember that it is not necessary to fold under an edge that is covered by another piece.

THREAD: We use cotton-covered polyester thread for appliqué and always match thread color to the fabric piece being sewn down.

POSITIONING APPLIQUÉ SHAPES: For precise placement of appliqué design elements, use the templates and removable marker to draw the shapes on the background fabric. Use the outlines as placement guides. Pin or baste the pieces in place and use a blind hemming stitch to sew them to the background fabric.

CIRCLES: To make circles (such as flower centers) perfectly round, cut a piece of stiff paper exactly the size of the flower center template, i.e., the finished size. Run a basting thread around the fabric circle, in the seam allowance. Place the paper circle on the wrong side of the fabric and pull the basting thread to draw the fabric around the paper. You may press if you wish. After you appliqué the circle in place, cut away the base fabric and remove the paper.

REVERSE APPLIQUÉ: Reverse appliqué is turning back one fabric to reveal another fabric. When making templates for reverse appliqué, you must cut out the inner shapes as well as the outline. The material under the inner shape will be exposed by the reverse appliqué. To make an underlay for an appliqué, cut a second piece of fabric slightly smaller than the top piece. Appliqué the larger shape, positioning the underlay beneath it. Cut the inner shapes, being sure to add a seam allowance. Clip the seam allowance of the inner shape as needed to turn it under with your needle as you appliqué. The raw edges of the underlay will be hidden by the appliqué piece (Figure 5).

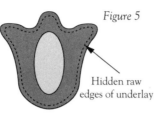

Figure 5

Hidden raw edges of underlay

TRIMMING AWAY BASE FABRIC: If the background fabric shows through any of the appliqué pieces, or if you plan quilting that will run over any appliqué pieces, you should cut the base fabric away to eliminate fabric shadows or unnecessary thickness. Generally speaking, if the appliqué involves several layers, the background fabric should be trimmed from behind the first appliqué pieces that are sewn down. When the next layer is added, base fabric behind those pieces is removed and so on. Sometimes, this base fabric is part of another appliqué piece, and sometimes, if appliqués overlap, only portions of the layers can be trimmed away. To trim, work from the wrong side of the block. With embroidery or appliqué scissors, carefully trim the background fabric from under the appliqué, leaving a scant ¼" seam allowance. Take care not to cut into the appliqué.

MAKING CURVED HANDLES FROM BIAS STRIPS

HANDLE STYLES: Many of the basket designs in this book have curved handles. These are made from bias strips folded in thirds and appliquéd to the handle section of the block. If the basket also has flowers or other contents, the handle is generally

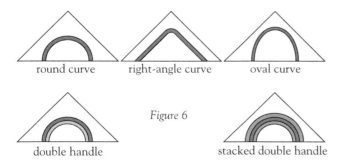

round curve   right-angle curve   oval curve

Figure 6

double handle   stacked double handle

appliquéd first. Although our photographs and illustrations may show a particular style or curve of handle with a certain basket, you can experiment and change the handles as you wish. Some handle options are shown in Figure 6.

HANDLE PLACEMENT GUIDES: You will need to make a special template to use as a placement guide for curved basket handles. You can sew the basket portion of the block first, then work with the handle. Make the placement guide by following the steps shown in Figure 7. On tracing paper, draw and then cut out a pattern of the triangle that is the handle section of the block. Fold the paper pattern in half. Sketch the handle style you desire on one half of the folded paper. Then, flip the paper over and complete the handle by tracing the curve you've drawn on the other half. Check to see that the handle will fit in well with your basket.

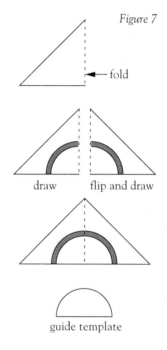

Figure 7

← fold

draw   flip and draw

guide template

Make a "half-moon" placement guide template that follows the bottom edge of the curve. If you are making many blocks for a quilt, the guide should be made of thin plastic or cardboard. For a single block, use the paper as a template.

Use the placement guide to mark a placement line for the lower, or inner, edge of your bias handle on the handle section of the quilt block.

HANDLE LENGTH: A handle for a 12" block basket requires a length of bias not longer than 20"; a 6" block basket needs approximately 10" of bias. To see exactly how long the bias should be, use a measuring tape set on edge to measure the curve of your handle placement guide. Suggested handle lengths are given in the appliqué basket section of this book for some of the appliqué baskets that have bias handles.

GENERAL
INSTRUCTIONS

HANDLE WIDTH: Handle width is also a matter of choice. For a narrow, delicate-looking handle, cut bias 1" wide. For a sturdier-looking handle, cut bias 2½" wide. For 6" blocks, we generally use 1" wide bias for handles. For 12" blocks, use wider bias. Experiment with width. One option is a double handle of two different widths, the narrower placed over the wider.

PREPARING HANDLE STRIPS: You may make continuous bias for basket handles if you wish, but we prefer handles with no seams. An easy way to make bias strips for handles is to use a plastic right-angle triangle to mark a 45° angle on your fabric (Figure 8). Next use a clear plastic ruler to mark cutting lines parallel to the first drawn line (Figure 9).

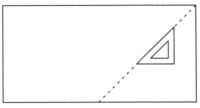

Figure 8

Another way to mark bias strips to is fold a corner of the fabric in, keeping the top raw edge and the selvage parallel to the straight grain of the fabric. Lightly press the 45° fold (Figure 10).

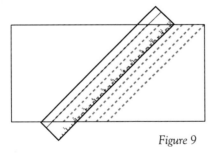

Figure 9

Then, open out the fabric and use a clear ruler to mark parallel cutting lines.

To prepare the bias strips for appliqué, fold

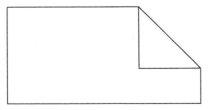

Figure 10

each one in thirds. The raw edge underneath should be hidden by one of the top folded edges. You can do the folding with an iron or by finger-pressing and thread basting.

Baste or pin the prepared handle piece onto the triangular handle section of the block, keeping the

bottom folded edge of the handle exactly on the marked placement line. Join the handle section to the basket section of the block with the handle just basted in place, then appliqué. Use a blind hemming stitch to appliqué the handle to the background fabric. Always appliqué the inner curve first, then the outer curve (Figure 11).

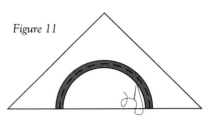

Figure 11

NOVELTY HANDLES: Use your imagination to devise different kinds of handles for basket blocks.

Some options are the use of rickrack, ruffled eyelet beading, ribbon-wrapped bias and striped fabric bias.

For a woven handle, use a removable marker to mark the curve on the handle section of the block. Make small marks on the curve where the loops will cross. Work with thin bias. For the French Basket (see page 106), we used bias cut ⅝" wide. Using two pieces of prepared bias, lap the folded strips over and under along the placement line, pinning or basting in place as needed (Figure 12). Appliqué, sewing first the inner curves, then the outer curves.

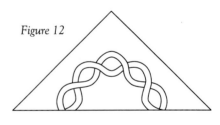

Figure 12

See photographs and illustrations throughout this book for handle ideas.

FLOWERS AND OTHER BASKET FILLERS

If you are making a block that has flowers or fruit and leaves, look carefully at the block illustration to see how the block is constructed. Sometimes these basket fillers are added to the top (handle section) of the block before that piece is sewn to the bottom (basket section) of the block. Sometimes a leaf or flower comes over the edge of the basket and is added after the handle and basket sections are joined.

The bunny and kitten included in this book are examples of appliqués added after the basket is complete (pages 23 and 53). The Springtime Basket (page 39) has appliquéd flowers on the basket itself – those pieces are added last, after the sections are joined, so you don't have to hold stretchy bias edges as you appliqué.

When appliquéing flowers and leaves and other basket contents, always work from background to foreground in the design and trim away the lower fabric as you layer. (See *Tips on Appliqué*, page 10.) Also, feel free to experiment with leaf and flower patterns throughout this book to create your own bouquet or design other filler styles yourself.

WOVEN APPLIQUÉ BASKETS

See page 114 for general instructions.

BIAS FOR STEMS AND VINES

For short stems, such as in Basket of Lilies (page 85), cut bias strips as you would for basket handles. For long vines, such as the French Basket Cameo Wall Quilt border (page 106), make 1" wide continuous bias.

Press or baste the bias in thirds, making sure the underneath raw edge is hidden by one of the top folds. Baste the vines to the background fabric. Appliqué the vines using a blind hemming stitch, stitching the inner curves first, then the outer curves.

QUICK-PIECING TECHNIQUES

CHAINING: If you do your patchwork with a sewing machine, you will save time (and thread) by sewing "chains" of patchwork units. Once you have cut out the fabric pieces for a patchwork block, lay them right side up, just as they will appear in the finished block. Then pick up and sew, right sides together, as many pieces as you can, running them through the machine one unit after another without

cutting thread. Then snip the units apart, press them and return to the sewing machine to add more pieces to the growing sections of the block. Piecing diagrams in each section of the book will help you decide how to construct the units.

ASSEMBLY-LINE SEWING: Assembly-line sewing is similar to chaining in that you feed patchwork pieces into the sewing machine one unit after another, without cutting threads. This technique is helpful when you are making a quilt that has a number of identical blocks. Once you have made a sample block, mass produce the rest of the blocks by joining the same pieces for all the blocks before adding other pieces. Cut the chains apart and then add more pieces. Remember that your patchwork will look best if seams are pressed before they are crossed by other seams.

TRIANGLE-SQUARES: Basket designs are often made with small triangles. Traditionally, these triangles were marked and cut individually and joined to form squares ("triangle-squares") wherever possible in the design.

Cherry Basket (Figure 13), for example, has 10 triangle-square units. The traditional construction method is fine if you are making only one or two blocks. But, if you are making blocks for a quilt, you will need hundreds of triangle-squares, and you will find the following technique a definite time-saver for producing accurate triangle-square units. The units produced will include the needed ¼" seam allowance. With this method, only one fabric need be marked.

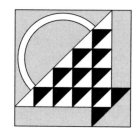

Figure 13

Step 1: First determine what size you want the *finished* triangle-square to be. Using the 12" Cherry Basket as an example, you'll need a 2" finished square (Figure 14). Now add ⅞" to the desired finished size, which will make it 2⅞".

finished triangle square

Figure 14

Step 2: Lay your two triangle-square fabrics *right sides together*, lighter colored fabric on top. Working with fabric pieces larger than 18" x 22" may be unwieldy.

Step 3: Mark a 2⅞" grid of squares on the wrong side of the lighter fabric, using a reliable see-through ruler and a pencil or permanent pen (Figures 15 & 16).

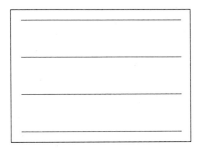

Figure 15

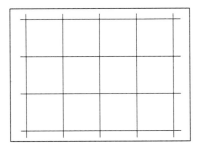

Figure 16

Step 4: Next, draw diagonal lines through your grid as shown in Figure 17. If you have drawn your grid carefully and accurately, your diagonal lines will go cleanly through every corner.

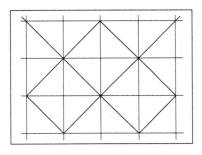

Figure 17

Step 5: Now you are ready to sew. Take an exact ¼" seam on *both* sides of every diagonal line. Follow the arrows to sew continuously (Figure 18). When you have sewn all the lines, cut the sewn pieces apart, cutting on every pen line. You get two identical units from every grid square drawn.

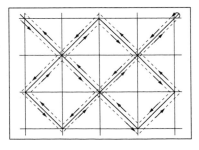

Figure 18

Step 6: These seams must be pressed before you proceed. Trim points (Figure 19). Check size of triangle-squares.

Figure 19

APPLYING THE TRIANGLE-SQUARE METHOD FOR A QUILT: Analyze the block to see how many triangle-square units of each fabric combination it has. Multiply this number by the number of blocks you need for the quilt. For example, the Cherry Basket shown in Figure 13 has 10 triangle-square units per block. If your quilt has, let's say, 12 blocks, then 10 triangle-squares x 12 blocks = 120 triangle-squares needed for the quilt. Mark and sew enough fabric pieces to produce 120 triangle-squares. It doesn't hurt to have a few extras.

CHECKERBOARDS: Squares in patchwork are traditionally marked and cut individually and then added to triangle-squares and other shapes to make a pattern. Sometimes when many squares combine in a repeated pattern, you can speed up the piecing process by quick-piecing squares. This method involves sewing long strips of fabric together in specific sequences, cutting them into strip sets and then combining the different strip set units to make a particular checkerboard pattern. This technique is applicable for the Triple Irish Chain Quilt (pages 22 and 36) and for the Checkerboard Basket (page 23) or Bow-Knot Basket (page 77), especially if you are using the same block in quantity for a quilt.

First, examine the pattern of squares you wish to construct and analyze its make-up. A simple pattern, such as the Nine-Patch, divides as shown in Figure 20.

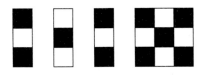

Figure 20

Once you have identified the rows of squares, use a heavy duty plastic ruler and rotary cutter to cut strips that are ½" wider than the finished size of the squares. For a 2" finished square, the strips should be 2½" wide.

Form the needed strip combinations by placing strips right sides together and sewing with a ¼" seam. Combinations for the Nine-Patch example are shown in Figure 21.

Figure 21

Press seam allowances to one side. Now, position your ruler perpendicular to the sewn strips and cut strip units that are the same width that the strips were cut (2½").

DIAGONAL SETS

Most basket blocks look best in a quilt when set on the diagonal. Set straight, the baskets tip over to one side. Diagonal setting lets the baskets stand up realistically. Figures 22 and 23 show sample setting diagrams for the alternate set (Figure 22: alternating design blocks with solid fabric blocks) and the solid set (Figure 23: design blocks only).

Figure 23

Figure 22

DIAGONAL MEASUREMENT: Planning a diagonal set is a bit more challenging than a straight set. To figure the size of a quilt with a diagonal set, you must know the diagonal measurement of the square block you are using. This measurement is referred to as D in Chart I on the next page.

The easy way to calculate the diagonal measurement (D) of a square is to multiply the length of the side of the square by 1.41.

For example, a 12" square has a diagonal measurement of 16.92"; that is, 12" x 1.41 = 16.92". Round this number off to the nearest ⅛". (It is probably easiest to work in decimals rather than fractions.) The diagonal measurement for a 12" square rounds off to 17". When in doubt, round off to the larger fraction.

Use the diagonal measurement of the block with the formulas in Chart I on page 16 to figure the dimensions of a diagonal set quilt. This chart shows examples worked out for 6" and 12" blocks used in a three block by four block diagonal set.

Chart I.
Diagonal Set Quilt Size (Example: 3-Block by 4-Block Set)

Length of side of block (B)	Diagonal Measurement of block B x 1.41 =D	Width of quilt W x D = width	Length of quilt L x D = length
6"	6"x 1.41 = 8.5"	3 blocks x 8.5" = 25.5"	4 blocks x 8.5" = 34"
12"	12" x 1.41 = 17"	3 blocks x 17" = 51"	4 blocks x 17" = 68"

Chart II.
Numbers and Types of Blocks Needed for Diagonal Set

Number of blocks in width and length	Alternate Set Number of design blocks W x L	Number of plain blocks (W − 1) x (L − 1)	Solid Set Number of design blocks + number of plain blocks	Number of half-block triangles 2(W − 1) + 2(L − 1)
3 x 4	3 x 4 = 12	(3 − 1) x (4 − 1) =6	12 + 6 =18	2(3 − 1) + 2(4 − 1) =10
4 x 5	4 x 5 = 20	(4 − 1) x (5 − 1) = 12	20 + 12 = 32	2(4 − 1) + 2(5 − 1) = 14
4 x 6	4 x 6 = 24	(4 − 1) x (6 − 1) = 15	24 + 15 = 39	2(4 − 1) + 2(6 −1) = 16

Chart III.
Sashing Stripes/Squares in a Diagonal Set
(Example: 3 x 4 set with 3" sashing)

Number of inches sashing adds to quilt	Number of sashing strips needed	Number of sashing squares needed
W x S x 1.41 = increase in width L x S x 1.41 = increase in length	W x L x 4	W(L + 1) + L(W + 1)
3 x 3" x 1.41 = 12¾" 4 x 3" x 1.41 = 17"	3 x 4 x 4 = 48	3(4 + 1) + 4(3 + 1) = 31

CHART KEY:
W = number of blocks in width of quilt
L = number of blocks in length of quilt
D = diagonal measurement of square
S = finished width of sashing
B = length of side of finished block (without seam allowance)

Note: Some numbers are rounded to nearest whole fraction.

NUMBERS & TYPES OF BLOCKS NEEDED: Quilts set on the diagonal are made up of square blocks, half-block triangles set into the four sides and quarter-block triangles for the corners. There are always four quarter-block triangles for corners, but the number of half-blocks will vary depending on the make-up of the quilt.

The formulas to figure block types needed for a quilt are given in Chart II on page 16. They will work for any diagonal set.

SETTING PIECES FOR DIAGONAL SET QUILTS: You can choose one of two methods for making the setting pieces (plain blocks, half-block setting triangles and quarter-block corner triangles) for diagonally set quilts. Instructions for both methods follow. If you use the template method, your setting pieces will have marked sewing lines. The quick-cutting method produces setting pieces with seam allowances included, but no sewing lines.

Template Method: For the *setting squares,* draw a square on graph paper the exact finished size of your quilt block. Make a template this size. Use the template to mark the setting squares for your quilt. Add seam allowances on all four sides before cutting. For the *half-block setting triangles,* divide the square template in half diagonally as shown (Figure 24). Use the template to mark the large setting triangles, placing the hypotenuse (longest side) of the triangle parallel to the lengthwise or crosswise grain of the fabric so that the outside edges of your quilt top will not be stretchy bias. Add seam allowances on all three sides before cutting. For the *quarter-block corner triangles,* divide the side triangle template in half as shown in Figure 24. Use the smaller template to

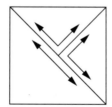

Figure 24

mark the four corner triangles. Place the short sides (the legs) of the triangles on the straight of the grain. Add seam allowances on all three sides before you begin cutting.

Quick-Cutting Method: For the *setting squares,* add ½" to the finished size of your block. Use a rotary cutter, heavy duty plastic ruler and cutting mat to cut the needed number of setting squares. The quick-cutting method for the *half-block setting triangles* involves cutting four triangles at a time by dividing a large square of fabric both ways diagonally, as shown in Figure 25. The first dimensions are for quilts with 12" blocks, with dimensions for 6" blocks in parentheses. To figure how many large squares you need to cut, count the number of setting triangles in your quilt and divide by four. If the number does not come out even, round off to the next highest number and simply discard the extra triangles.

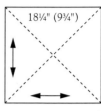

Figure 25

The quick method for *quarter-block corner triangles* involves cutting two squares of fabric and then dividing them in half diagonally one way to produce the needed four triangles. The dimensions to use for quilts with 12" blocks are given in Figure 26, with dimensions for 6" blocks in parentheses.

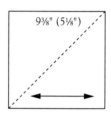

Figure 26

SETTING BLOCKS TOGETHER IN A DIAGONAL SET: Sewing blocks together for a diagonally-set quilt is like sewing straight-set blocks, except that the blocks are joined in diagonal rows instead of straight rows. Figure 27 illustrates the construction rows of a three-block by four-block setting. As you sew the rows together, be

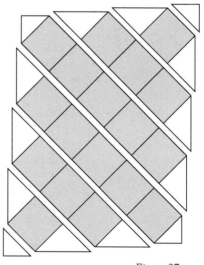

Figure 27

careful handling the bias edges of the half-block and quarter-block triangles.

SASHING IN A DIAGONAL SET: Sashing strips separate the blocks and are generally used with a solid set, where every block is a design block. The quilt size is increased when sashing strips are used.

The diagonal set with sashing is sewn together like a regular diagonal set, only sashing strips are added between blocks in a row and between rows of blocks.

You can use solid sashing or insert sashing squares at the intersections of the crisscrossing lines. If you are using sashing squares, the squares at the outer edges of the quilt are trimmed to triangles after the top is sewn together.

The formulas given in Chart III on page 16 will help you to calculate how much the use of sashing will increase the width and length of a quilt and will determine how many sashing strips and squares you need for any diagonal set. The number and size of the half-blocks and quarter-blocks remain the same as for the block-to-block diagonal set.

For sashing without sashing squares, the size formula in Chart III remains the same. You must cut enough short strips to insert one between each pair of blocks as you construct the rows of blocks (refer to Figure 27). Then, cut a strip equal to the longest side of each row and sew these strips between pairs of rows as you complete construction of the quilt top.

MITERING BORDERS

If you add fabric borders to a quilt, these borders will generally look best with mitered corners. Mitered corners are sewn at a 45° angle seam from the inner to the outer edge of the border.

When starting a project with mitered borders, it is wise to cut the borders from your yardage before you cut the pieces for patchwork or appliqué. Cut border strips the width you desire plus ½" for the two ¼" seam allowances.

Border strips must be cut the full length of the side of the quilt plus twice the width of the border plus 2"-3" extra for "accident insurance." Borders are marked for the exact size before they are sewn to the quilt as explained below. To find the exact size for a mitered border, including seam allowances, measure the full length of the side of the quilt to be bordered. Measure through the middle of a project rather than along an outside edge since an outer edge may have stretched from handling.

An alternate way to determine the exact length to mark a border is to work with the mathematical measurement of the side to be bordered. To do this, count the number of blocks in the length or width of the quilt. Multiply by the size the block *should* be (i.e. 6", 12" or the diagonal). Be sure to include sashing if the quilt is sashed. This way, you know the exact measurement that the side *should* be. Add seam allowances to this measurement before marking the border fabric. When you add the border, you will be able to take up fabric that may have stretched and you will avoid unattractive "ruffled" borders.

To mark a border strip the exact size for mitering, measure and mark on the fabric strip the exact length of the side to be bordered (Figure 28). Next,

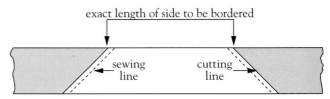

Figure 28

mark a 45° angle line across each end of the border strip. You can use an artist's plastic angle or you can make a 45° template by cutting a cardboard square in half diagonally. The 45° angle lines you draw are the cutting lines. Once you have marked these lines, mark a sewing line ¼" to the inside.

Pin the strip to the side of the quilt, matching centers and right sides. Match the sewing lines at the ends of the border strip to the ¼" sewing lines at the corners of the quilt top. Pin well all along the side, evenly distributing any extra fullness of the top that may have been caused by the fabric's stretching. If you do have fullness that needs taking up, be sure to sew with the excess fabric on the bottom – the feed dogs of your machine take up the slack for you. Begin and end the seam with a backstitch.

In this manner, add all borders to the sides of the quilt. Then, match the 45° angle sewing lines on adjacent borders. Sew miters from inner to outer edge. Press seams. Borders should fit precisely as marked; if they do not, adjust as necessary, then trim away excess border fabric from seam.

Multiple borders such as those on the Eight-Basket Child's Quilt (pages 38 & 50) are sewn together in long strips first. Measure and mark the angles on the sewn fabric and sew the borders on as described above.

QUILTING

Quilting is a small running stitch that holds the layers of fabric, batting and backing together. It enhances an appliqué or patchwork design, adding dimension and interest to the overall effect of any quilted piece.

Quilting thread is available in many colors and is stronger than regular thread. Quilting needles ("betweens") are shorter and stronger than other sewing needles. We always use a hoop or frame to hold our work for quilting. A hoop is not necessary for a very small project, but is strongly recommended for other projects.

Work from the center of a project out to the edges. The three layers (top, batting and backing) should be well basted before the quilting begins.

To start quilting, knot a single thread about 18" long. Working from the top of the quilt, run the needle through the layers, coming up where you wish to begin the quilting stitches. Tug gently to pull the knot through the top and into the batting.

To end quilting, make a loop-knot in the thread and slide the knot down to about ¼" above the surface of the quilt. Put the needle in the quilt top where the next stitch would be and bring the needle out about one needle's length away. Pull the knot through the top into the batting. It's helpful to put your thumbnail on the knot to help pop it into the batting.

MARKING: It's generally best to mark fabric for quilting before laying the batting and lining under it. Quilting designs can be marked in a number of ways. If the fabric is light-colored enough that you can see through it, lay the fabric over the drawn quilting design and simply trace with removable marker (tailor's chalk, soapstone pencil or an artist's silver pencil). Some dark fabrics can be traced through a light table or sunny window. Any fabric can be marked with a commercial or homemade stencil. We have included several fully drafted quilting designs for the projects in this book.

QUILTING BASKET PATTERNS. To quilt the small triangles in many basket patterns, quilt in the sequence diagrammed in Figure 29. The small feather

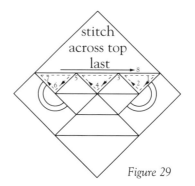

Figure 29

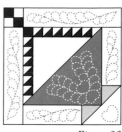

Figure 30

designs given on page 127 will work well in the side rectangles of the basket patterns in this book (Figure 30). A good motif for an alternate plain block is a quilted basket grid marked with a transparent ruler (Figure 31), which was used in the Twelve-Basket Cradle Quilt shown on page 52.

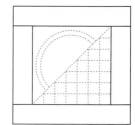

Figure 31

QUILT BINDINGS

Fabric estimates and instructions for quilts and wallhangings in this book include material for straight grain binding. Cut binding strips and borders first to ensure that you don't come up short of fabric, then proceed to cut the patchwork pieces. Binding strips are generally cut 2½" wide. Sew the strips together end to end to reach the length needed to go around the quilt, plus 12" extra for mitering corners. Sewing diagonal seams will distribute the bulk of the seam allowance better than straight seams. Fold the strip in half lengthwise, wrong sides together and press.

If you prefer to use bias binding, French fold bias (bias folded double before it is applied) is most durable. (For instructions on making continuous bias binding, consult any home sewing guide.) Bias binding is applied in the same manner as straight grain binding, for which instructions are given below.

Another binding option is to cut the backing fabric wide enough to allow for folding a hem over the top of the quilt, which is then hand stitched in place.

BINDING A QUILT

1. Place the raw edges of the folded binding strip even with the outer edge on the right side of the quilt top. (Excess batting and backing will be trimmed after the binding is machine stitched in place.) Choose an inconspicuous spot to begin, away from a corner.

2. Fold the beginning raw end of the binding back ½" and stitch. Machine stitch through all layers, sewing ¼" from the raw edge of the binding. See instructions on mitering corners below.

3. When you get back to the beginning point, continue sewing the binding ½" beyond the fold edge of the beginning binding. Clip off any remaining binding. That first fold conceals the ending raw edge when the binding is turned (Figure 32).

Figure 32

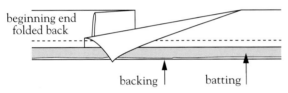

beginning end
folded back

backing   batting

4. When binding is sewn, trim away any excess batting and backing. It's best not to trim these layers perfectly flush with the binding edge, but to leave a little to fill the binding nicely when turned.

5. Turn binding to the back of the quilt so that it covers the machine stitching and hand stitch the folded edge to the quilt back with a blind hemming (appliqué) stitch. Use a few pins just ahead of your stitching to keep the binding in place.

MITERING BINDING CORNERS:

1. When approaching the corner to be mitered, *stop stitching ¼" from the bottom edge* of that corner. Backstitch, clip threads and remove the work from the sewing machine.

2. Fold the binding straight up, away from the corner, to form a 45° angle fold (Figure 33).

3. Bring the binding straight down in line

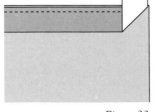

Figure 33

with the next side to be sewn. A fold is formed even with the previously sewn side. Begin stitching the next side at the top fold of the bias, stitching through all layers as shown in Figure 34. Miter each corner in this manner.

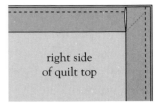

right side
of quilt top

Figure 34

4. To finish miter on the back of the project, blind stitch right up to the corner formed by the machine stitches (Figure 35). Fold binding over next side. Take a stitch or two in the miter fold to secure it. Then, proceed along the next edge of the quilt (Figure 36).

backing side
of quilt

Figure 35

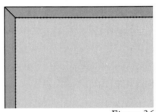

Figure 36

HANGING QUILTS

TABS: Tabs, which allow the insertion of a decorative rod or dowel, are an attractive way to hang a small project. The tabs are spaced evenly across the top of the wallhanging and are generally placed no more than 12" apart. Hanging tabs are basted in place before the binding is sewn on and are usually made of the same fabric as the binding. (See examples on pages 49, 61 & 81.)

First, decide how many tabs will look best for your project. Cut a strip of fabric (on the straight grain) 4½" wide by the total length needed, allowing 6" length for each tab. For example, cut a strip 4½" x 30" for five tabs.

Fold the strip in half lengthwise, right sides and raw edges together. Sew along the length of the strip, taking a ¼" seam. Center the seam on the back of the strip and press the seam allowances open. Turn right side out and press again. Cut the long strip into the required number of 6" tabs.

Fold each tab in half, with the seam to the inside. Each tab is now 2" x 3" folded.

Space the tabs evenly across the top of the hanging on the back side, matching the raw edges. Pin or baste the tabs in place. Sew binding to the right side of the project; this stitching secures the tabs. Bring the binding to the back side and hand stitch in place. Fold the tabs up and tack them to the top edge of the binding so it won't roll forward when the project is hung.

SLEEVE: The best way to hang a quilt or wallhanging is with a hanging sleeve. A hanging sleeve is a tube of fabric sewn to the back side of a quilt at the top through which a hanging rod or dowel is inserted, distributing the weight of the quilt evenly. Many museums, galleries and quilt exhibitions request a hanging sleeve on quilts to be shown.

To add a 4" wide hanging sleeve to a quilt before binding it, cut a strip of muslin or fabric to match the quilt back that is 8½" wide and 1" shorter than the width of the quilt. Turn ½" to the wrong side on each narrow end of the strip and stitch next to the raw edge. Then, fold the strip in half lengthwise, matching wrong sides and raw edges and press. The strip is now 4¼" wide and 2" shorter than the top of the quilt.

Pin or baste the raw edges of the sleeve even with the top raw edge on the back of the quilt, centering the sleeve 1" in from each side. Sew the binding to the right side of the quilt, securing the sleeve to the quilt as you sew. Turn the binding to the wrong side to cover the raw edges; hand stitch the binding to the back of the quilt through the sleeve. Hand stitch the folded bottom edge of the sleeve to the back of the quilt.

A sleeve can also be added to a quilt that is already bound. Cut a fabric strip for the sleeve 5" wide and 1" shorter than the width of the quilt. Turn ½" to the wrong side on each short end and machine stitch next to the raw edge. Press ½" to the wrong side on each long side of the strip. The strip is now 4" wide and 2" shorter than the top of the quilt. Center it just below the binding on the top edge of the back of the quilt. Hand stitch both long folded edges to the quilt back.

If the bottom of the wallhanging flares out when hung, you can add a sleeve at the bottom as well. A dowel or length of screen molding inserted in the sleeve will help the quilt to hang evenly.

Basket blocks can be used for a range of projects, including these basket pocket tote bags. Instructions begin on page 75.

A 3", 6" or 12" block can be the perfect center for a patchwork album cover. See page 93 for instructions.

A 6" basket block can be the focal point for the back of a strip vest.

Quick-piecing techniques make this Triple Irish Chain quilt a faster, easier project than it looks. Here, 6" Valentine Baskets make the "plain" blocks interesting. Any 6" block can be used. Instructions for the quilt begin on page 36.

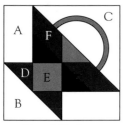

Bread Basket

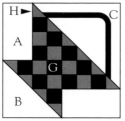

Checkerboard Basket

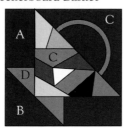

Crumb Basket

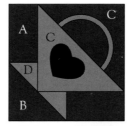

Valentine Basket

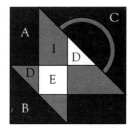

Simple Basket

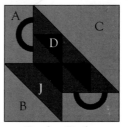

Garden Basket

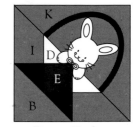

Bunny Basket

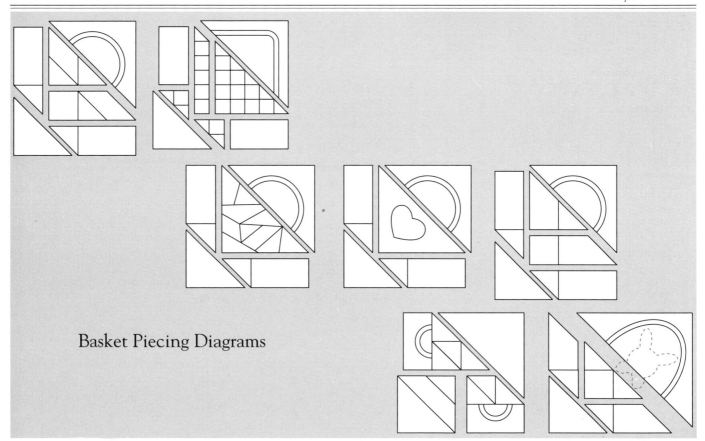

Basket Piecing Diagrams

BASKETS

6" Blocks
add ¼" seam allowances

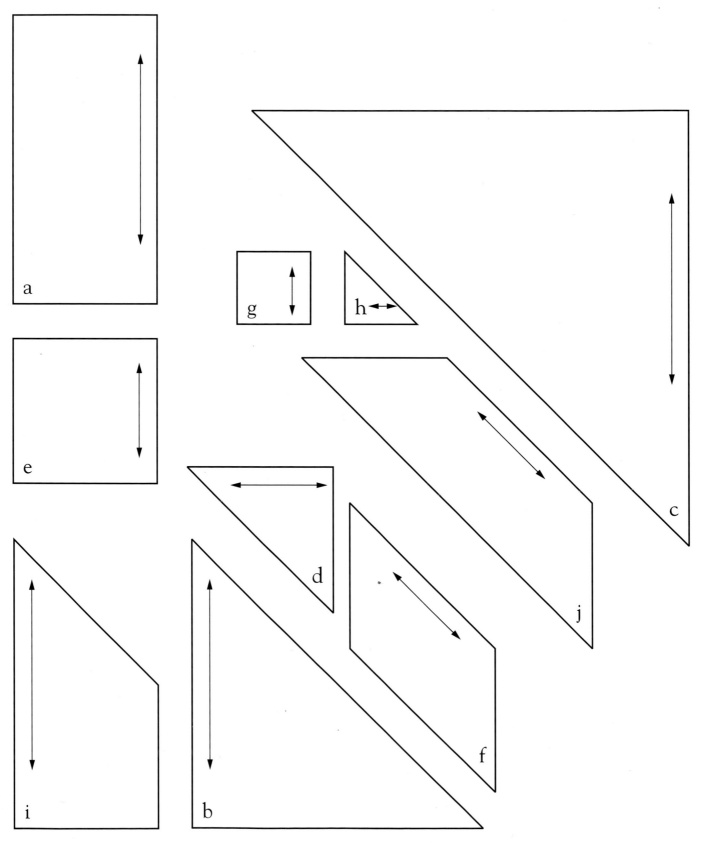

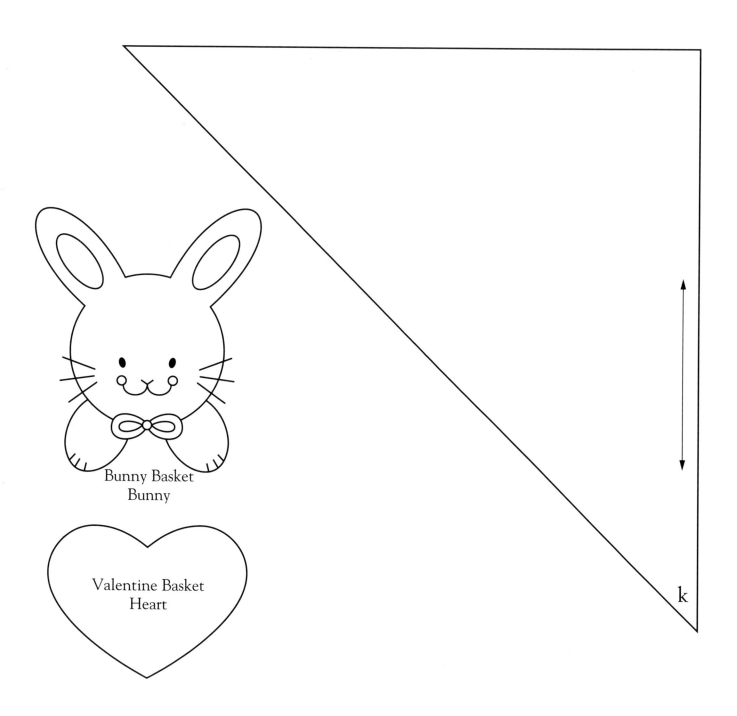

Bunny Basket
Bunny

Valentine Basket
Heart

k

4-PATCH
BASKETS

12" Blocks
add ¼" seam allowances

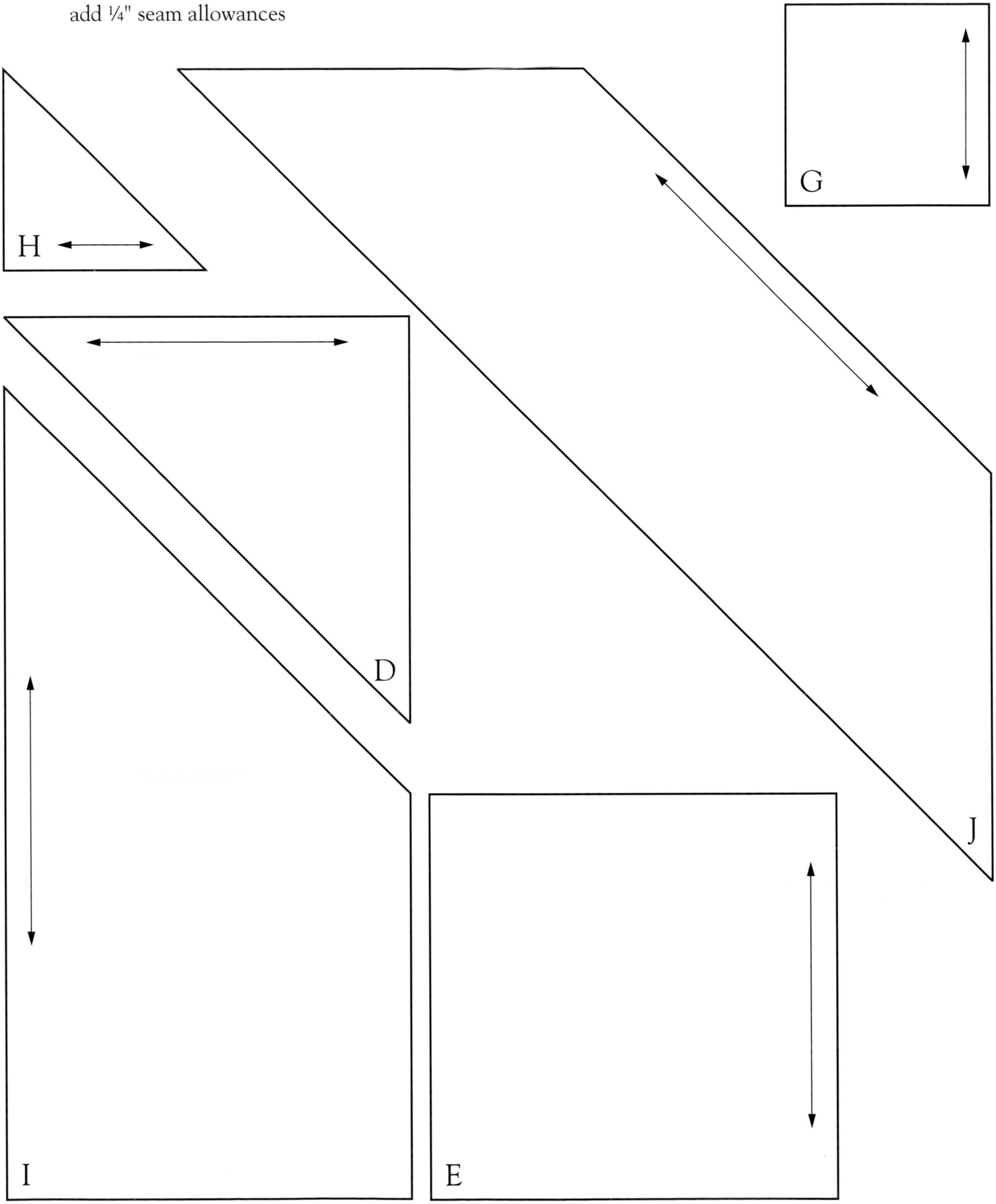

H

G

D

I

E

J

12" Blocks (continued)
add ¼" seam allowances

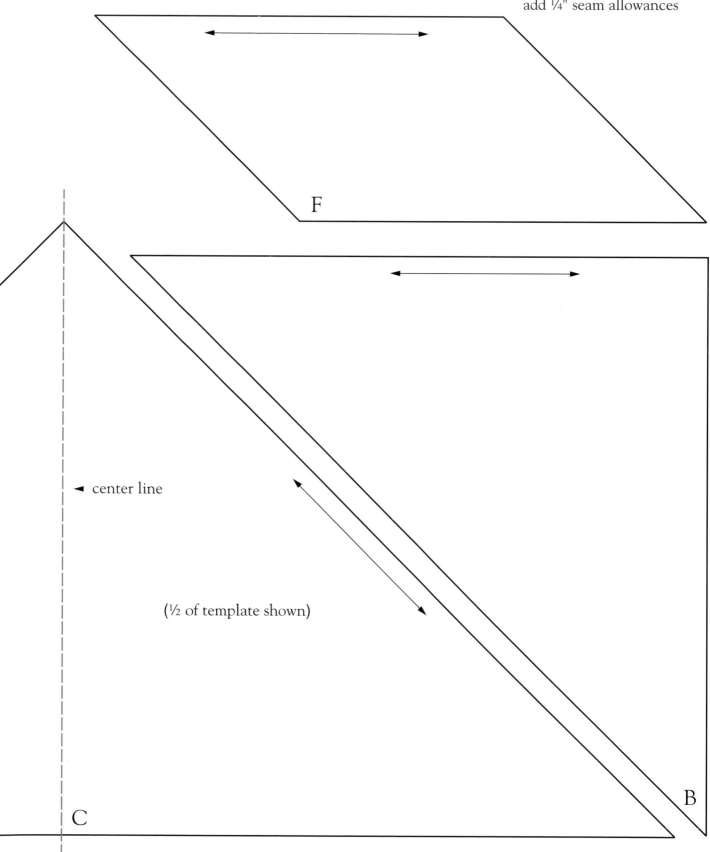

F

center line

(½ of template shown)

B

C

4-PATCH
BASKETS

12" Blocks (continued)
add ¼" seam allowances

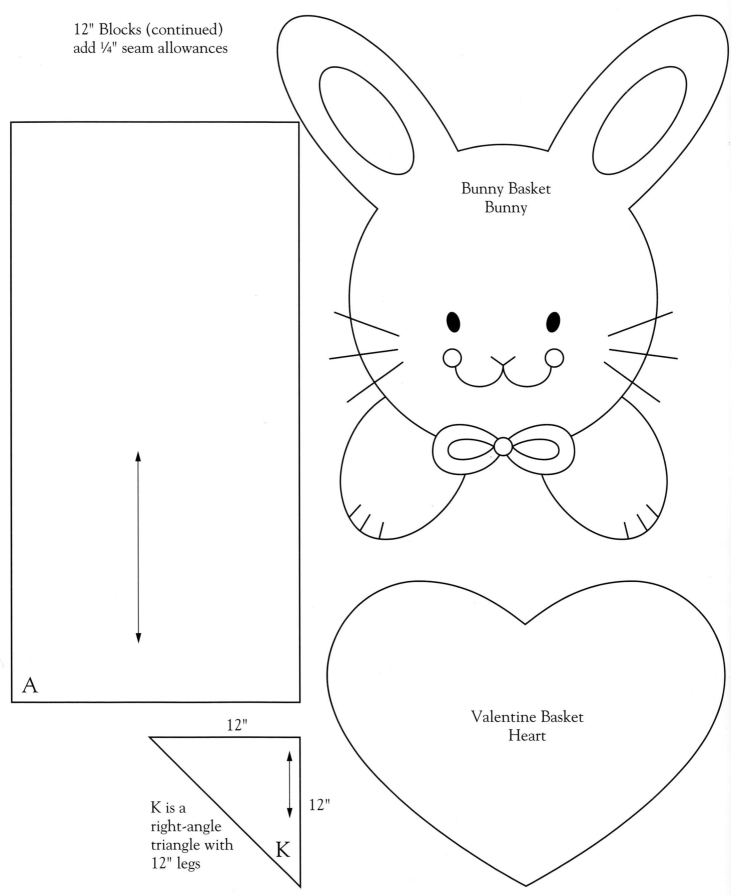

A

12"

12"

K is a
right-angle
triangle with
12" legs

K

Bunny Basket
Bunny

Valentine Basket
Heart

NINE-BASKET WALL QUILT

Finished Size: 34½" x 34½"
6" Valentine Basket Block

The quilt pictured below uses the 4-Patch Valentine Basket, but you can use any 6" block in this layout. The Cake Stand Wall Quilt, shown on page 48, and the Nine-Block Sampler, shown on page 99, are set in the same manner but have different border treatments.

YARDAGE

1 yard Fabric #1 (red print) for middle border, setting pieces and heart appliqués
¾ yard Fabric #2 (blue print) for outer border, background of basket blocks and binding
½ yard Fabric #3 (natural print) for inner border and baskets
1 yard backing fabric
Batting, larger than 34½" x 34½"

CUTTING INSTRUCTIONS

Make templates using Patterns a, b, c, and d included in the 6" Block Patterns on page 24 and the heart pattern on page 25.

Always cut borders and binding strips from yardage before cutting smaller pieces for patchwork. Measurements given for borders and binding are 2-3" longer than needed. Exact trimming will be done when the borders are sewn to the quilt top.

1. From Fabric #1 (red print), cut four 2" x 33" strips for middle border. Cut four setting squares, eight half-block setting triangles, and four quarter-block corner triangles. Refer to the general instructions, page 17, for instructions for cutting setting pieces.
2. From Fabric #2 (blue print) cut four 2½" binding strips across the fabric width. Cut four 2½" x 38" strips for the outer border.
3. From Fabric #3 (natural print), cut four 1½" x 31" strips for the inner border.
4. From the remaining fabrics, cut the pieces for nine Valentine Basket blocks.

SEWING INSTRUCTIONS

1. Make nine Valentine Basket blocks (or another 6" block of your choice). Refer to the general instructions for tips on appliqué and basket handles.
2. Set the blocks together with the setting blocks, half-block triangles and quarter-block corner triangles as shown in the photograph. The inner quilt should measure 26" x 26", including seam allowances.
3. Refer to the general instructions, page 18, on adding and mitering borders.
4. Quilt as desired. The quilt above is quilted in the ditch in the basket blocks and borders. The setting pieces are quilted with a grid of one-inch squares.
5. After quilting, add binding as described in the general instructions.

CRUMB BASKET WALL QUILT

Finished Size: 23" x 23"
6" Crumb Basket Block

The wall quilt shown right and in the diagram on page 32 uses the 6" Crumb Basket block and features crumb-pieced borders. Instructions are for using that block. You can use any 6" block in this setting but will need to purchase ¼ yard of border fabric to cut four 3½" x 17½" border strips in place of the crumb pieced borders if you don't wish to use crumb piecing.

CRUMB PIECING

Crumb piecing, which is similar to crazy patchwork, is worked with cotton fabrics on a freezer paper foundation. The technique is also called "save all patchwork" and "piece as piece can" in some regions of the United States.

TO MAKE A CRUMB BASKET:

1. Make a finished-size template for 4-Patch Block Pattern c (for a 6" block) or C (for a 12" block). Use the template to mark and cut a finished-size triangle from plastic-coated freezer paper.
2. Cut a small fabric scrap with straight (not curved) sides. The scrap may be a square, rectangle, triangle, or any other straight-sided shape. Using a dry iron set at the wool setting, press the scrap onto the approximate center of the shiny side of the paper triangle as shown in Figure 1.

3. Position a second fabric scrap atop the first scrap with right sides facing and the edges aligned on one side. With the sewing machine stitch length set at 12-15 stitches per inch, take a ¼" seam along the aligned sides as shown in Figure 2. Sew the length of the bottom fabric piece, stitching through both fabrics and the paper.

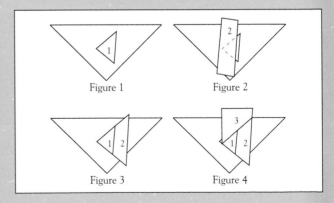

Figure 1

Figure 2

Figure 3

Figure 4

4. Open out the top fabric and finger press the seam. Trim the piece so the sides form straight lines with the

YARDAGE

1 yard Fabric #1 (blue print) for setting square and triangles, basket handles, base triangles, border corner squares and binding

¼ yard Fabric #2 (cream print) for background of basket blocks

Scraps of 10-12 assorted print fabrics to coordinate with above fabrics

¾ yard backing fabric

Plastic-coated freezer paper

Batting, larger than 23" x 23"

CUTTING INSTRUCTIONS

Make templates using Patterns a, b, c and d, which are included in the 6" Block Patterns found on page 24.

1. From Fabric #1 (blue), cut three 2½" wide binding strips across the fabric width. Cut one setting square, four half-block triangles and four quarter-block corner triangles, referring to the general instructions on page 17. Cut four 3½" squares for the border corners, eight basket base triangles (Template d) and four 1" x 9" bias strips for the basket handles.

2. From Fabric #2 (cream), cut background pieces for four 6" Crumb Basket blocks (using Templates a, b and c).

3. From freezer paper, using Template c, cut four finished-size paper triangles and measure and cut four 3" x 17" paper border strips to use as foundations for crumb piecing.

first piece as shown in Figure 3. Press the piece to the freezer paper to hold the loose edges in place.

5. In the same manner, add a third fabric along one side of the first two pieces as shown in Figure 4. Continue to add pieces in this manner, working around the center piece, until the paper triangle is covered with fabric. Build seam allowances around the paper triangle by leaving at least ¼" of fabric extending all around the paper. When the piecing is complete, turn the paper triangle over and trim the fabric so the seam allowances are a consistent ¼".

6. Combine the crumb pieced triangle with the other pieces to form the block. Stitch the block together, using the edge of the paper as a seam guide. Carefully tear the paper from the wrong side of the completed block. The point of a seam ripper is a handy tool to loosen the paper in small areas.

CRUMB-PIECING TIPS

1. Because it is difficult to remove paper from narrow seam allowances, work crumb piecing on finished-size paper foundation pieces rather than pieces with seam allowances included. Remember to build ¼" wide fabric seam allowances around finished-size paper foundations.

2. Working around the beginning piece in either a clockwise or counterclockwise direction rather than adding pieces to all one side keeps the patches more even in size.

3. When adding pieces, sew only the length of the underneath piece to avoid creating an L-shaped opening that can't be filled in a continuous straight seam. You may want to use pins to mark the starting and stopping points for your stitching.

4. To trim a new patch so it forms a straight line with a previously sewn patch, turn the paper triangle over so it is wrong side up. Fold the paper back along the edge of the previous fabric piece; trim the new piece even with the edge of the folded paper.

FINISHING THE WALL QUILT

1. Add crumb-pieced borders to two opposite sides of the wall quilt. Sew border corners to each end of the two remaining borders; sew the borders to the quilt. Machine stay-stitch in the outer edge seam allowance along the border pieces; carefully remove the paper backing from the border strips.
2. Quilt as desired.
3. After quilting, add binding as described in the general instructions.

PATCHWORK INSTRUCTIONS

1. Make four 6" Crumb Basket blocks. Refer to pages 30-31 for crumb piecing instructions. See the general instructions on using bias for basket handles.
2. Refer to the wall quilt diagram above and sew the blocks together with the setting triangles and setting square. See the general instructions for diagonal sets on page 17.
3. Cover the paper border strips with crumb patchwork, making sure the crumb piecing extends ¼" beyond the edges of the paper on all sides, to provide seam allowances.

Crumb Basket Bed Quilt

CRUMB BASKET BED QUILT

Finished Size: 70½" x 91"
12" Crumb Basket

The Crumb Basket quilt shown on the cover uses the 4-patch Crumb Basket block. The diagram is opposite. Yardage and instructions are for that block, but any 12" block can be used.

YARDAGE

3¼ yards Fabric #1 (blue print) for borders and sashing strips

2¼ yards Fabric #2 (red print) for setting triangles, sashing squares and binding

2 yards Fabric #3 (natural solid) for background of basket blocks

¼ yard or scraps of 9-20 assorted print fabrics to coordinate with above fabrics for basket handles, basket base triangles and crumb patchwork

Plastic-coated freezer paper

5¼ yards backing fabric

Batting, larger than 70½" x 91"

CUTTING INSTRUCTIONS

Make templates using Patterns A, B, C and D, included in the 12" Block Patterns on pages 26-28.

Always cut borders and binding strips from yardage before cutting smaller pieces for patchwork. Measurements given for cutting borders and binding are longer than the exact length that should be needed to allow for any discrepancies in piecing. Exact trimming can be done when borders are sewn to the quilt top.

1. From Fabric #1 (blue), cut four 5" x 94" border strips and 48 sashing strips, each 3" x 12½".

2. From Fabric #2 (red), cut eight 2½" wide binding strips across the fabric width. Cut ten half-block setting triangles and four quarter-block corner triangles, referring to the general instructions on page 17. From remainder, cut 31 sashing squares, each 3" square.

3. From freezer paper, use Template C to mark and cut 18 finished-size triangles.

4. From Fabric #3 (natural), cut background pieces for 18 Crumb Baskets (using Templates A, B and C).

5. From the assorted print fabrics, cut 1¼" x 14" bias strips for 18 basket handles and matching pairs of D triangles for the basket bases.

PATCHWORK INSTRUCTIONS

1. Make 18 Crumb Basket blocks. Refer to pages 30-31 for crumb piecing instructions. See the general instructions for information on using bias for basket handles.

2. Set the blocks together with sashing strips and half-block and quarter-block triangles as shown in the diagram. Refer to the general instructions on diagonal sets, page 17. The inner quilt top should measure 62" x 82½", including seam allowances.

FINISHING THE QUILT

1. Refer to the general instructions for tips on adding and mitering borders.

2. The full-size quilting designs for the handle portion of the blocks and for the sashing strips are on page 34. Other quilting designs can be used.

3. After quilting, add binding as described in the general instructions.

BASKETS

Crumb Basket Bed Quilt
Quilting Design

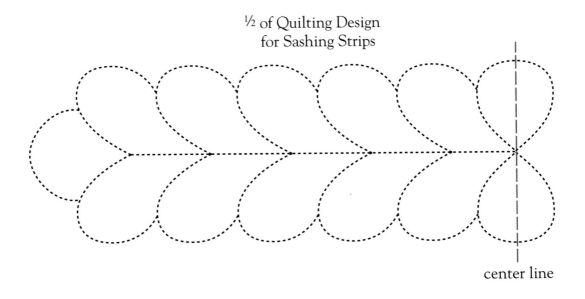

½ of Quilting Design
for Sashing Strips

center line

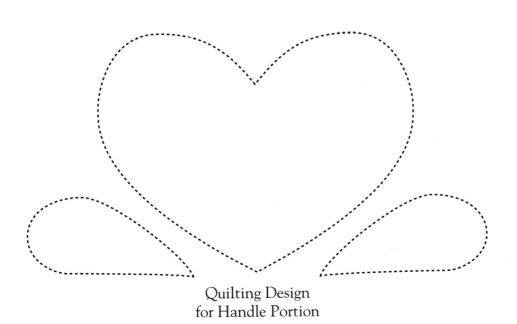

Quilting Design
for Handle Portion

SINGLE BASKET BIB

Finished Size: 9" x 12"
6" Bunny Basket Block

The bib pictured below features the 6" Bunny Basket block. Instructions are given for using that block, but any 6" block can be substituted.

INSTRUCTIONS

1. Make one 6" Bunny Basket block (or another block of your choice). Appliqué the bunny, by hand or by machine, after the patchwork is complete (see general instructions for appliqué, page 10). For hand appliqué, cut the head and paw sections separately, adding ¼" seam allowances.

2. Finish the basket with a handle of bias or rickrack.

3. Match batting to wrong side of one lining piece. Center basket block on batting diagonally as shown. Pin all layers well.

4. On the straight of the grain, cut 21 strips of coordinating fabric, each 1½" wide and up to 9" long.

5. Add framing strips to fill in corner areas. Starting on any side of the basket block, place the first strip right sides together with the block and raw edges even. Machine stitch through all layers (strip, block, batting and lining), taking a ¼" seam. Proceed around block clockwise until rectangle is filled, as shown.

6. Trim excess strip fabric. Fold bib in half lengthwise and cut out a small neck opening at the center top. Round off corners.

7. Baste eyelet on the right side of the patchwork bib, matching right sides and raw edges. Place extra lining rectangle on top, matching right sides with bib. Sew a ¼" seam from one side of the neck opening around to the other. Trim excess lining; clip seam allowance. Turn right side out through neck opening. Finish neck opening with bias strip.

YARDAGE

¼ yard pieces of four or more coordinating fabrics, or use scraps, for block and patchwork strips
Two pieces 9" x 12" fabric for lining
9" x 12" batting
1¼ yard pre-gathered eyelet trim
10" of rickrack or bias for basket handle
30" double fold bias for ties

TRIPLE IRISH CHAIN QUILT

Finished Size: 80" x 100"
6" Valentine Basket Block

The quilt shown on page 22 uses the 4-Patch Valentine Basket. The instructions are for using that block, but you can use any 6" block in this quilt.

This quilt is designed for a double bed. It should fit a standard 54" x 75" mattress with a pillow tuck and a 13" drop. The quilt is made of 63 blocks, each 10" square. Thirty-one of the squares are "basket blocks," consisting of a 6" basket block framed by a patchwork of 2" squares. The remaining 32 quilt blocks are "checkerboard" blocks, a five-patch patchwork of 2" squares.

YARDAGE

2⅞ yards Fabric #1 (dark brown print) for patchwork and binding
4½ yards Fabric #2 (medium brown print) for patchwork and borders
2 yards Fabric #3 (light brown print) for patchwork
1¾ yards Fabric #4 (muslin or natural solid) for patchwork and background of basket blocks
1 yard blue print for baskets and handles
¼ yard dark brown print for basket hearts or use scraps from fabric listed above
6 yards backing fabric
Pre-cut batting larger than 80" x 100" or the equivalent yardage (6 yards, 48" wide) for piecing the batting

CUTTING INSTRUCTIONS

Make templates using Patterns a, b, c and d in the 6" Block Patterns on page 24 and the 6" Heart Pattern on page 25.

Always cut borders and binding strips from yardage before cutting smaller pieces for patchwork or setting blocks. Measurements given for cutting borders and binding are 2-3" longer than the exact length that should be needed to allow for any discrepancies in piecing. Exact trimming can be done when borders are sewn to the quilt top.

1. From Fabric #1 (dark print), cut four binding strips, 2½" x 103". From the remainder, cut 18 strips for the patchwork, each 2½" x 45". Cut all pieces on lengthwise grain.
2. From Fabric #2 (medium brown print), cut two border strips 5½" x 104" and two border strips 5½" x 84". From the remainder of this fabric, cut 32 strips for the patchwork, each 2½" x 45". Cut all pieces on the lengthwise grain.
3. From Fabric #3 (light brown print), cut 24 strips 2½" x 45", cutting on the crosswise grain.
4. From Fabric #4 (muslin), cut eight strips 2½" x 45", cutting on either grain.
5. From the remaining fabrics, cut 31 sets of basket pieces and handles.

PATCHWORK INSTRUCTIONS

1. Make 31 Valentine Basket blocks, or another 6" basket of your choice. Refer to general instructions on making curved handles and on chaining and assembly-line sewing.
2. The 6" basket blocks are completed with the addition of surrounding patchwork squares. Use the quick cutting and piecing techniques described in the general instructions. Make four of each of the strip combinations shown (Figure 1) each 45" long. Press seams toward the center strip.

Figure 1

Strip Set #1

Strip Set #2

3. From each sewn set, cut 2½" sections.

4. Add the three-square units to top and bottom of the basket blocks. Then add five-square units to each side (Figure 2).

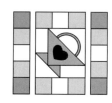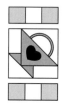

Figure 2

5. The same quick-piecing techniques are used to create 32 checkerboard blocks. Using your cut strips, make four strip sets of both Set #3 and Set #4 as shown below. You need only two of Set #5 (Figure 3). When pressing these strips, it is best to press seams toward the center on Sets #3 and #5 and toward the outer edges on Set #4 – this distributes bulk when strips are joined and prevents lumpy patchwork.

Figure 3

Strip Set #3   Strip Set #4   Strip Set #5

6. Cut each strip set into 2½" units as shown.
7. Each checkerboard block is made with two units from Sets #3 and #4 and one unit of Strip Set #5. Match seams carefully as you sew units together (Figure 4).

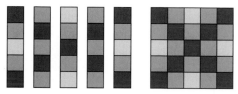

Figure 4

8. Refer to diagram for correct block positioning. Combine the 63 completed blocks in seven vertical rows of nine blocks each, matching seams carefully. The checkerboard and basket blocks alternate as shown.
9. Join the seven rows together. Finished size of quilt top should now equal approximately 70½" x 90½".

FINISHING THE QUILT

1. Refer to general instructions for tips on adding and mitering borders.
2. The quilt shown on page 22 features a basket weave quilting design. Quilting design is optional.
3. When quilting is complete, add binding as described in the general instructions (page 20).

5-PATCH
BASKETS

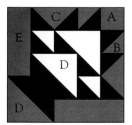

A May Basket

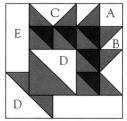

Grape Basket

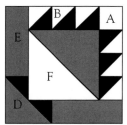

Cake Stand

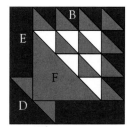

Flowerpot

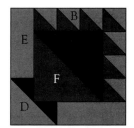

Fruit Basket

Springtime Basket

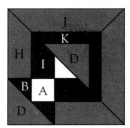

Dresden Basket (6" only)

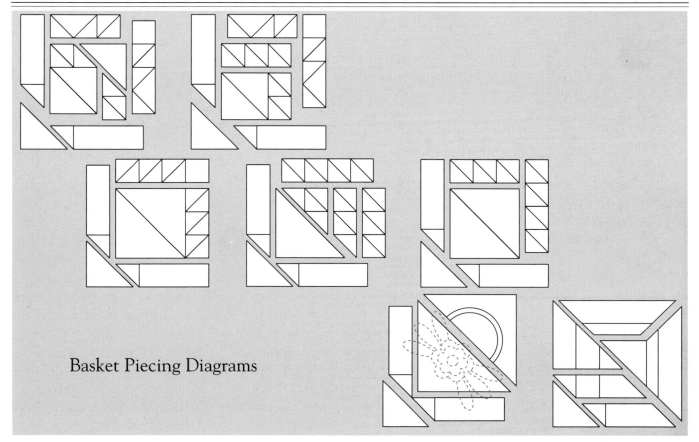

Basket Piecing Diagrams

6" Block Patterns
add ¼" seam allowances

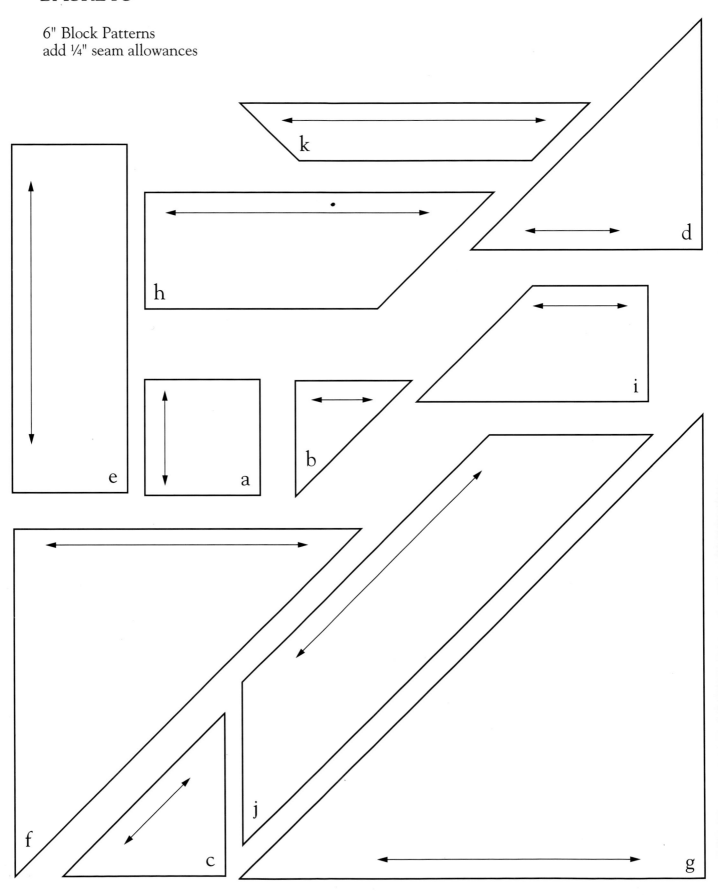

12" Block Patterns
add ¼" seam allowances

Flower and leaf patterns
for 6" and 12" Springtime
Baskets are on page 51.

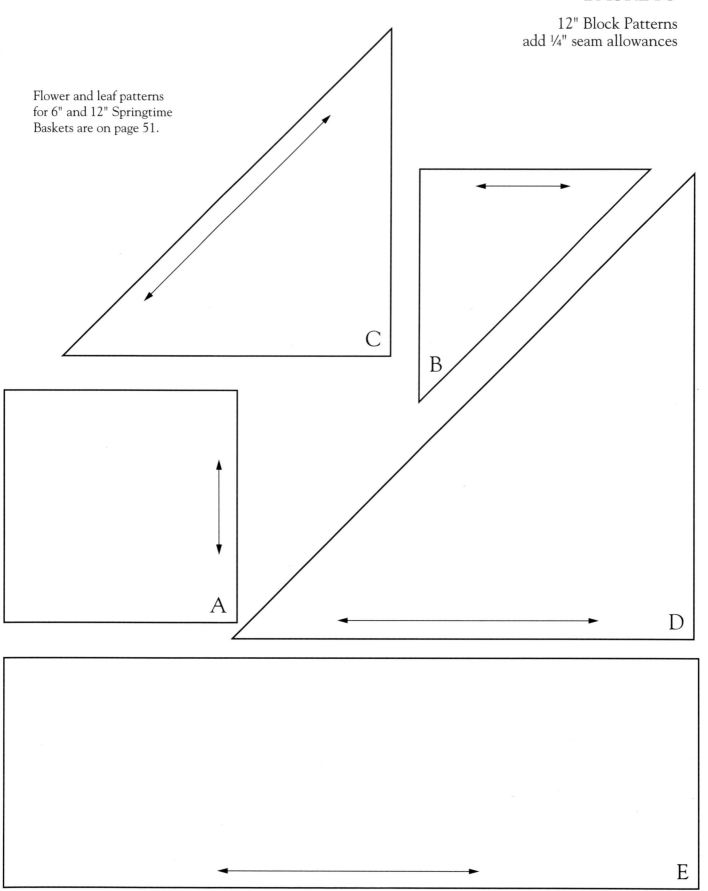

C

B

A

D

E

12" Block Patterns
add ¼" seam allowances

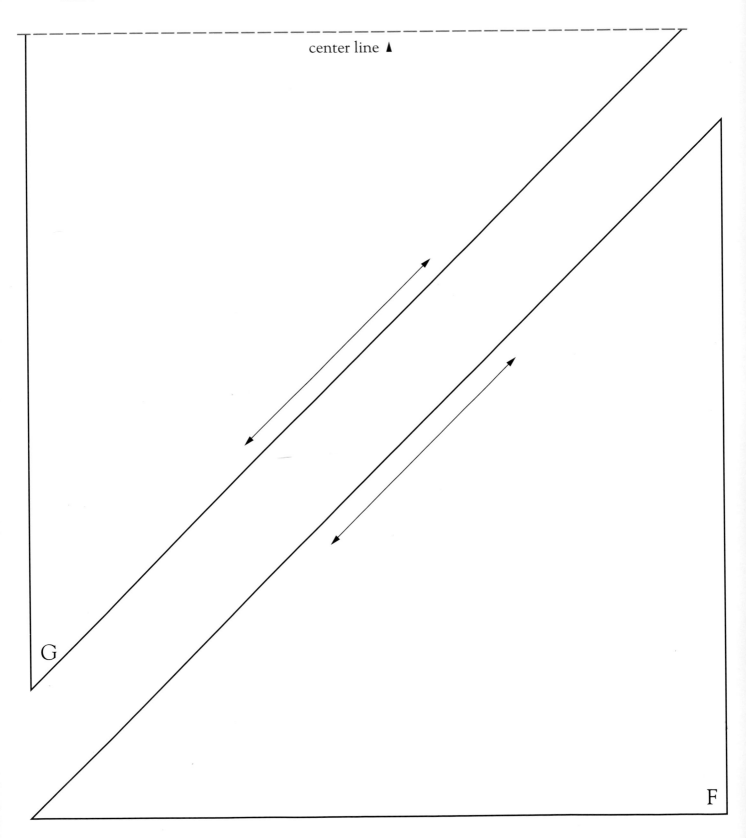

center line ▲

G

F

Quilting Designs for
Scrap Flowerpot Bed Quilt

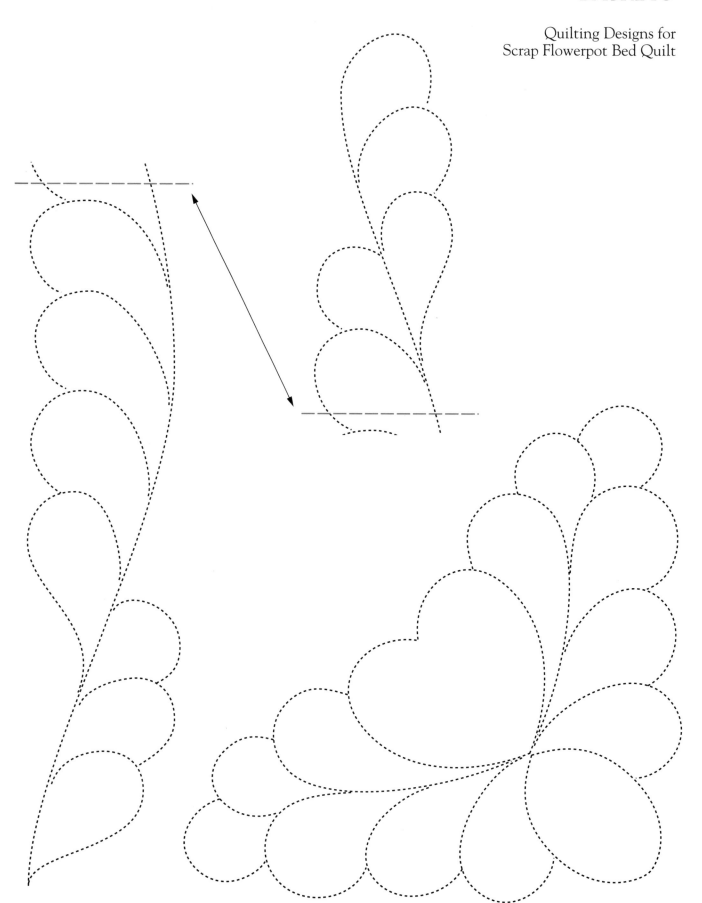

SCRAP FLOWERPOT BED QUILT

Finished Size: 70½" x 91"
12" Flowerpot Basket Block

The quilt shown on page 45 features the Flowerpot Basket block. The instructions are for using this block, but any 12" block can be used. The Flowerpot Baskets are pieced from 18 different printed fabrics combined with a light-colored background print. To speed the piecing process for the small triangles, instructions are written for quick piecing using the triangle-squares method.

YARDAGE

3¾ yards Fabric #1 (dark purple) for borders, sashing strips and binding

1½ yards Fabric #2 (tan print) for half-block triangles, quarter-block triangles and sashing squares

2½ yards Fabric #3 (white and blue print) for basket background

¼ yard pieces or scraps (at least 9" x 24" each) of 18 different printed fabrics for basket patchwork

5½ yards backing fabric

Batting, larger than 70½" x 91"

CUTTING INSTRUCTIONS

Make templates for Patterns D, E, and F, which are included in the 12" Block Patterns on pages 41 and 42.

Always cut borders and binding strips from yardage before cutting smaller pieces for patchwork or setting blocks. Measurements given for cutting borders and binding are at least 2-3" longer than the exact length needed to allow for any discrepancies in piecing. Exact trimming can be done when borders are sewn onto the quilt top.

1. From Fabric #1 (purple), cut eight 2½" wide binding strips across the fabric width. Cut four border strips, each 5" x 94". Cut 48 sashing strips, each 3" x 12½".

2. From Fabric #2 (tan), cut ten half-block setting triangles and four quarter-block corner triangles, referring to general instructions, page 17. Cut 31 sashing squares, each 3" square.

3. From Fabric #3 (white and blue print), use Template E to cut 36 rectangles and use Template D to cut 18 triangles. From the remainder, cut 18 rectangles, each 8" x 14" to make triangle-squares and individual B triangles.

4. From each of the 18 scrap fabrics, cut one 8" x 14" rectangle for the triangle-squares and individual B triangles. From the remainder of each scrap fabric, use Template F to cut one triangle (18 total).

TRIANGLE-SQUARE INSTRUCTIONS

1. Pair an 8" x 14" rectangle of Fabric #3, right sides together, with a scrap-fabric rectangle. On the wrong side of the Fabric #3 rectangle, draw a 2 x 4 grid of 3¼" squares. Draw a diagonal line through six of the squares, exactly as shown in Figure 1. Pin the two fabrics right sides together.

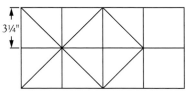

Figure 1

2. Machine stitch *exactly* ¼" on both sides of the diagonal lines, starting at the upper left of the grid. Sew continuously around the grid; then sew on the other side of the diagonal lines. Figure 2 shows the sewing pattern. Leave the two unmarked squares unsewn to cut into single triangles.

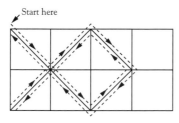

Start here

Figure 2

3. Cut the grid apart into squares. Cut all squares, including the unsewn squares, diagonally into two triangles. Open out the seams of the sewn squares and press the seam allowances to one side. Trim the excess seam allowances (triangle tips) as shown in Figure 3. You will have four single triangles (B triangles) of each fabric and 12 triangle-squares.

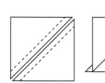

Figure 3

4. Pair the remaining Fabric #3 and scrap fabric rectangles and make triangle-squares and single triangles. Following these instructions will make a few more triangle-squares and single triangles than you will actually need for the baskets, allowing you more choice when combining triangle-squares in each basket block.

PATCHWORK INSTRUCTIONS

1. Make 18 Flowerpot basket blocks. Use a variety of triangle-squares in the top portion of the baskets, but match the base (B) triangles to the large basket (F) triangle to unify each basket.

2. Refer to the quilt diagram on page 44 and lay out the blocks in a pleasing arrangement. Set the blocks together with sashing strips, half-block triangles, and quarter-block corner triangles as shown in the diagram. Refer to general instructions on diagonal sets, page 17. The quilt top should measure approximately 62" x 82½", including seam allowances.

FINISHING THE QUILT

1. Refer to the general instructions for tips on adding and mitering borders.

2. Full-size patterns for the feathered quilting designs used in the sashing strips and the large F triangles on the quilt shown below are given on page 43. Quilting designs are optional.

3. After quilting, add binding as described in the general instructions.

PADDED WICKER BASKET COVERS

Finished Size: Varies
6" State Fair Block

The padded basket cover shown right uses a 6" State Fair block (included in the diamond section, page 85). Any 6" block may be substituted.

YARDAGE

Scraps of various fabrics for patchwork
Lining fabric
Polyester filling and/or batting
Ribbon ties (optional)
Ruffle or pre-gathered lace (optional)

INSTRUCTIONS

1. Every basket is different, so you must make a pattern to fit the one at hand. Turn your wicker basket upside down on a large piece of paper; trace the outer rim. If the basket has a handle, place the basket at the edge of a table to draw each half – allow extra length for the width of the handle.
2. Use this paper pattern to cut a cover from cardboard. Trial check the fit of the cardboard cover on the basket. Adjust fit of the cardboard before proceeding.
3. Make one or more basket blocks. Add strip work or crazy patchwork (see photo above right) to make a fabric cover. When finished, the pieced fabric should be the same shape and size as the cardboard cover, plus ½" seam allowances on all sides.
4. A ruffle or pre-gathered lace is optional. If desired, baste ruffle or lace ¼" from edge of fabric cover, matching right sides.
5. Cut the lining fabric to the size of the cardboard, plus ½" seam allowances. Place the fabric cover over the lining, right sides together. Sew half way around the cover, taking a ¼" seam. The opening must be large enough to insert the cardboard piece.
6. Turn the fabric cover right side out. Insert the cardboard cover in the opening. Add loose polyester filling, if desired, to softly stuff the cover. Hand stitch the opening closed.
7. Ribbon ties may be added to fasten the cover to the basket handles.

BUTCHER APRON

Finished Length: 36"
6" Dresden Basket Block

The apron pictured below features the 6" Dresden Basket block. Instructions are given for using that block, but any 6" block can be substituted.

YARDAGE

1 yard sturdy fabric for apron (denim, canvas, etc.)
½ yard rose print for patchwork, binding
¼ yard scraps of blue and rust fabrics

INSTRUCTIONS

Make templates for Patterns a, b, d, h, i, j and k, which are included in the 6" Block Patterns on page 40.
1. Make five 6" Dresden Basket blocks.
2. On one block, baste under ¼" on the outside edges. Sew the remaining blocks end to end to make a 24½" long strip.

3. Cut the apron as shown below.

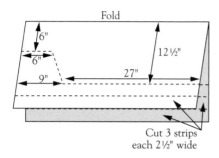

4. Two 2½" x 36" strips are for sashes. On these, press under ¼" on the two long sides and one end. Fold the strips in half lengthwise, matching wrong sides. Topstitch the three finished sides.

5. For the neck ties, follow the same procedure with the one remaining strip, but press under ¼" on all four edges of the strip. Topstitch all sides. Cut the finished strip in half to make two ties.

6. Center the prepared basket block on the apron bib. Appliqué it in place.

7. Position the sewn strip of blocks on the apron 6" from the bottom edge of the apron fabric, right sides together. A few pins will keep the strip smooth and straight. Taking a ¼" seam, sew the block strip to the apron. Smooth blocks to right side so that bottom edges of patchwork and apron match.

8. Pin sashes and ties to the wrong side of the apron, matching raw edges. Try on apron and adjust position of sashes and ties to fit.

9. Make 1¼" wide bias binding, cutting it from a 14" square. Machine stitch the bias to the right side of the apron, taking a ¼" seam. Turn the bias to the wrong side of the apron and finish by hand or machine topstitch.

For matching hot pads, make extra 6" blocks. For insulation, cut up old towels or use a double layer of cotton batting (polyester conducts heat). Cut a 6½" square of insulation for each pad and position it between the patchwork block and a 6½" square of backing material. Bind with bias. *Be very careful to heat-test any homemade hot pad before putting it to use!*

CAKE STAND WALL QUILT

Finished Size: 32" x 32"
6" Cake Stand Block

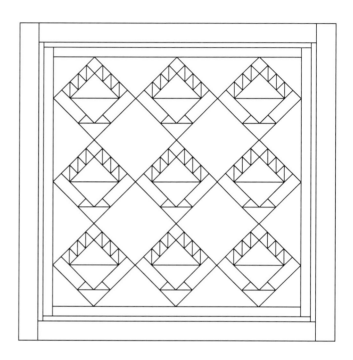

The yardage and instructions below are for the Cake Stand Wall Quilt shown on page 48, but you can use any 6" block in this layout. The Valentine Basket wall quilt, pictured on page 29, is the same nine-block setting, but has wider border strips. The sampler in the photograph on page 99 also has a three-by-three block setting.

YARDAGE

1 yard Fabric #1 (blue print) for outer border and setting pieces

¾ yard Fabric #2 (off-white solid) for patchwork, inner border and binding

¼ yard Fabric #3 (tan print) for middle border and patchwork

Scraps of approximately 23 different print fabrics for patchwork

1 yard backing fabric

Batting, larger than 32" x 32"

CUTTING INSTRUCTIONS

Make templates for Patterns a, b, d, e, and f, which are included in the 6" Block Patterns on page 40.

Always cut borders and binding strips from yardage before cutting smaller pieces for patchwork. Measurements for borders are longer than the exact length needed to allow for any discrepancies in piecing. Exact trimming can be done when borders are sewn to the quilt top.

1. From Fabric #1 (blue print), cut four 2½" x 35" outer border strips. Refer to the general instructions, page 17, and cut four setting squares, eight half-block setting triangles and four quarter-block corner triangles.

2. From Fabric #2 (off-white solid), cut four 2½" wide binding strips across the fabric width. Cut four 1½" x 30" inner border strips.

3. From Fabric #3 (tan print), cut four 1" x 31" middle border strips.

4. From the remaining fabrics, cut the necessary pieces for nine 6" Cake Stand blocks. Use a different combination of scraps for each block.

SEWING INSTRUCTIONS

1. Make nine 6" Cake Stand blocks. Refer to the general instructions for tips on patchwork.

2. Set blocks together with the setting pieces to make the inner quilt top, referring to the quilt diagram on page 47. The inner quilt top should measure 26" x 26", including seam allowances.

3. Sew a Fabric #2 border strip to the top and bottom of the quilt; trim even with the quilt. Sew the two remaining Fabric #2 border strips to the two opposite sides; trim. Add the Fabric #3 and Fabric #4 border strips in the same fashion. The completed quilt top should measure 32½" x 32½", including seam allowances.

4. Quilt as desired. The blocks on the Cake Stand Wall Quilt shown below are quilted in the ditch. The setting pieces are quilted in a grid pattern and the borders are quilted with a scroll pattern.

5. After quilting, add binding as described in the general instructions.

GOOSE CHASE BORDER WALL QUILT

Finished Size: 33½" x 33½"
12" Flowerpot Block

This project features four 12" Flowerpot Basket blocks set "tops in" and framed by a complementary Goose Chase border. Instructions are given for using the Flowerpot block, but this border treatment would work nicely with a four-block setting of any 12" block.

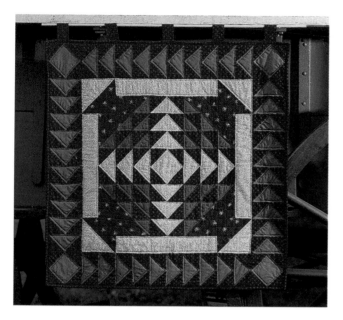

YARDAGE

1¼ yards small red print for blocks, borders, binding, tabs
½ yard blue pin-dot for blocks and border
½ yard white print for block background
¼ yard large red print for block patchwork
1 yard backing fabric
1 yard batting

INSTRUCTIONS

Make templates for Patterns B, C, D, E and F, which are included in the 12" Block Patterns on pages 41 and 42. Also make a template for Pattern L, at right. Patterns B, D, E and F will be used for the Flowerpot blocks and Patterns C, B and L will be used for the Goose Chase border.

1. Before cutting other pieces from the small red print fabric, cut four binding strips on the lengthwise grain, each 2½" x 40".
2. Make four 12" Flowerpot blocks (or another block of your choice). Sew them together into a four-block unit with the base of each basket at an outer corner.
3. For pieced border, make 40 of the Goose Chase units, using the B and C triangles given on page 41. Join units into four strips of 10 each (Figure 1).
4. Make four corner units as shown below, using B triangles and L squares (Figure 2).
5. Add a corner unit to each end of two border strips.
6. Sew the border strips without corners onto opposite sides of the four-block unit, matching center seams. Sew remaining border strips (with corners) onto remaining sides. Match seams at centers and corners.
7. Refer to general instructions to make hanging tabs (page 20), as well as for tips on quilting and binding.

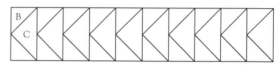

Figure 1

Figure 2

L

EIGHT-BASKET CHILD'S QUILT

Finished Size: 65½" x 88"
12" Springtime Basket Block

The quilt pictured on page 38 uses the 12" Springtime Basket block. Instructions are given for that block, but any 12" block can be used. This quilt is designed to fit a standard 39" x 75" twin-size mattress. It has no allowance for a pillow tuck. It allows a drop of approximately 13" on the end and at either side.

YARDAGE

4½ yards Fabric #1 (hot pink) for large flowers, inner and outer borders, sashing strips, binding
2⅜ yards Fabric #2 (bright green) for baskets, handles, middle border and sashing squares
1½ yards Fabric #3 (white print) for half-block triangles, quarter-block triangles and background of basket blocks
⅜ yard Fabric #4 (green check) for flower leaves
⅛-¼ yard each of pink check for inner flowers and pink/white print for flower centers or use scraps
5¼ yards backing fabric (to be pieced lengthwise)
Pre-cut batting larger than 65½" x 88".

CUTTING INSTRUCTIONS

Always cut borders and binding strips from yardage before cutting smaller pieces for patchwork or setting blocks. Measurements given for cutting borders and binding are 2-3" longer than the exact length that should be needed to allow for any discrepancies in piecing. Exact trimming can be done when borders are sewn to the quilt top.

Make templates for Patterns D, B, G and E, which are included in the 12" Block Patterns on pages 41 and 42. Also make templates for flower shapes and leaf shape for 12" blocks, found on page 51.

1. From Fabric #1 (hot pink), cut two binding strips, each 2½" wide x 4½ yards long. (These pieces are sewn end to end to make one continuous binding strip.) Cut four border strips, each 4½" wide x 90" long. Cut four more border strips, each 4½" x 68". Borders will be cut to the correct length when added to the top and mitered. From the remainder, cut 24 sashing strips, each 4½" x 12½". Use the scraps to cut pieces for basket appliqué.

2. From Fabric #2 (green), cut two border strips, each 2½" x 85", and two border strips 2½" x 60". Cut

17 lattice squares, each 4½" square. From the rest, cut pieces for eight baskets and handles.

3. From Fabric #3 (white print), cut six half-block triangles and four quarter-block triangles (see the general instructions, page 17). From the remainder, cut pieces for eight basket blocks.

4. Cut eight sets of appliqué pieces from the appropriate fabrics.

PATCHWORK INSTRUCTIONS

1. Make eight Springtime Basket blocks (or another 12" block of your choice). Refer to the general instructions for tips on appliqué, basket handles and chaining.

2. Set the blocks together with sashing strips, half-blocks and quarter-block triangles as shown in the diagram. Refer to the general instructions on diagonal sets, page 17. The finished size of the completed quilt top should now equal approximately 45½" x 68".

FINISHING THE QUILT

1. Refer to the general instructions for tips on adding and mitering borders.

2. The quilt shown on page 38 features a feathered flower quilting design in the sashing. The same design was adapted for the border corners and lattice squares. A full-size quilting pattern for this design is given (below). Other quilting designs can be used.

3. After quilting, add binding as described in the general instructions.

Flower and Leaf for 12" Springtime Basket
add ¼" seam allowances

Flower and Leaf for 6" Springtime Basket
add ¼" seam allowances

simplified flower shape

for 6" block

Quilting Design for Springtime Basket Quilt

center line ▶

The Twelve-Basket Cradle Quilt is a special gift for any new baby. It uses twelve 6" Kitten Basket blocks and features setting squares and triangles that are sashed to give a zigzag effect. Yardage requirements and instructions are on page 68.

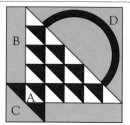

Cherry Basket

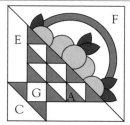

Orange Basket

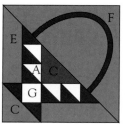

New York Basket

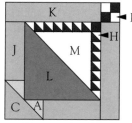

Hanging Basket

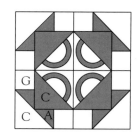

Tiny Baskets

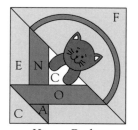

Kitten Basket

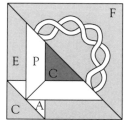

Parquet Basket

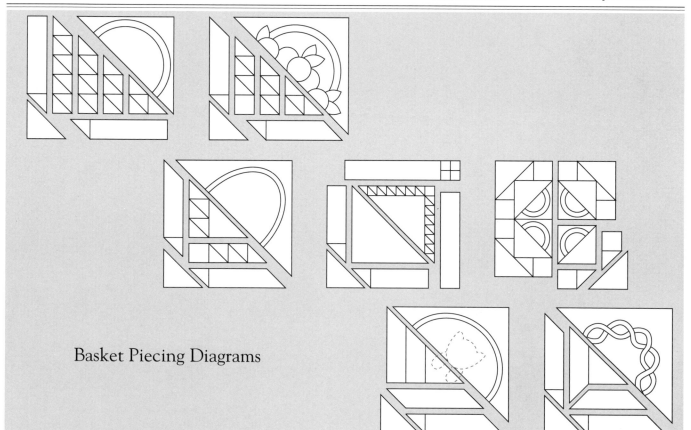

Basket Piecing Diagrams

6" Blocks
add ¼" seam allowances

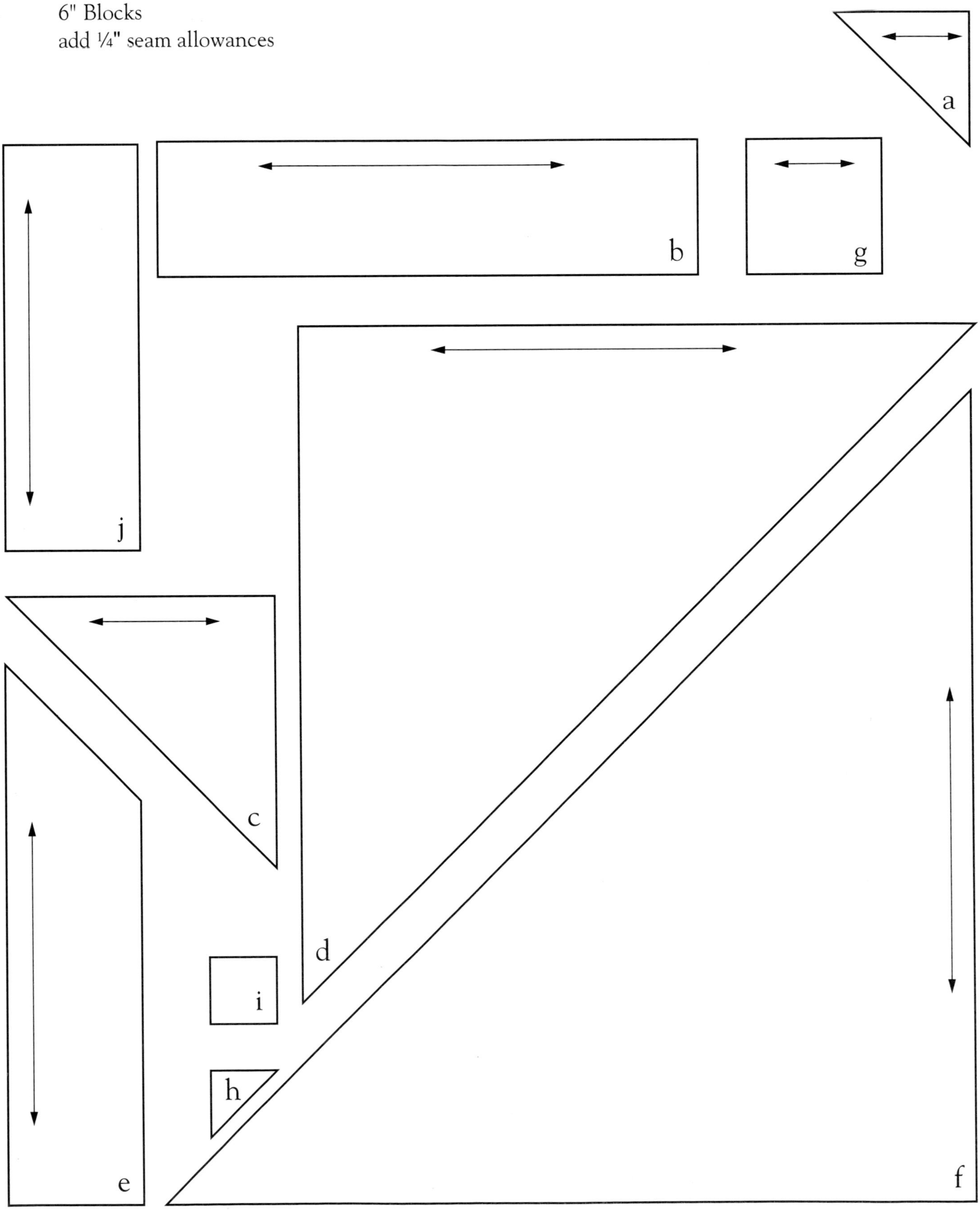

a

b

g

j

c

d

i

h

e

f

6" Blocks (continued)
add ¼" seam allowances

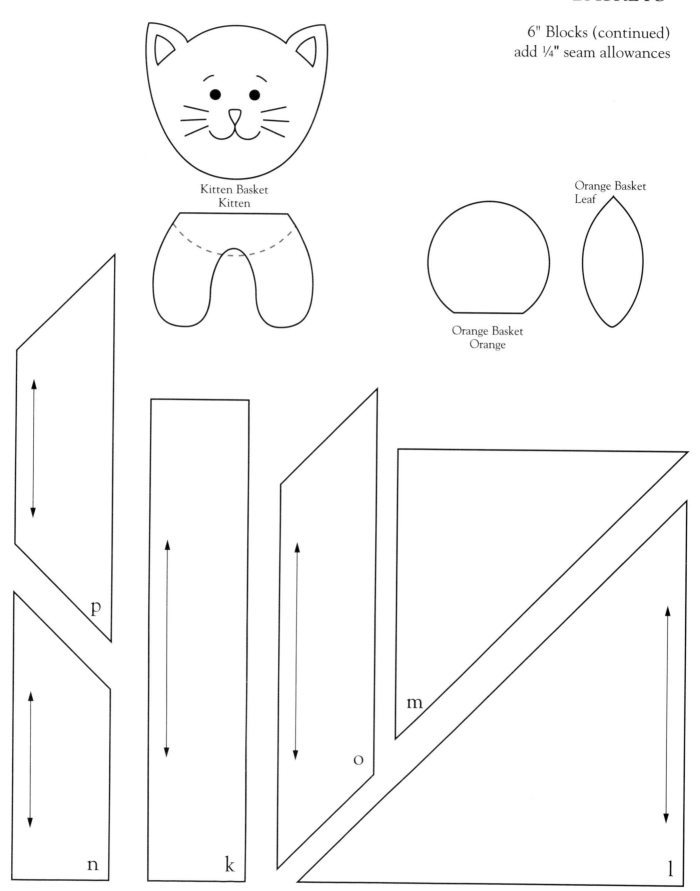

Kitten Basket
Kitten

Orange Basket
Leaf

Orange Basket
Orange

p

n

k

o

m

l

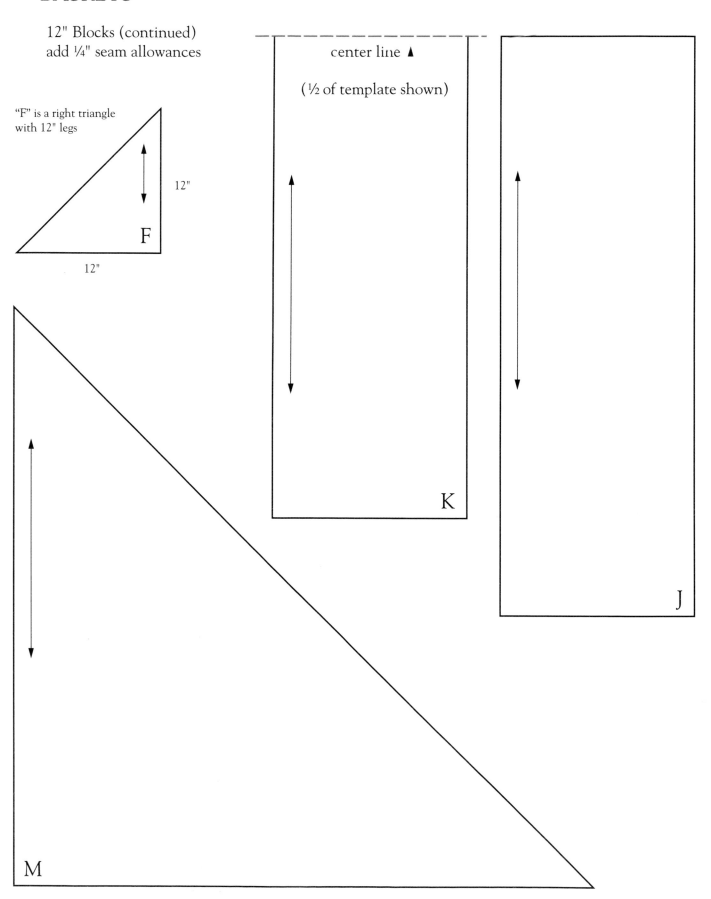

12" Blocks (continued)
add ¼" seam allowances

"F" is a right triangle
with 12" legs

12"

12"

F

center line ▲

(½ of template shown)

K

J

M

12" Blocks (continued)
add ¼" seam allowances

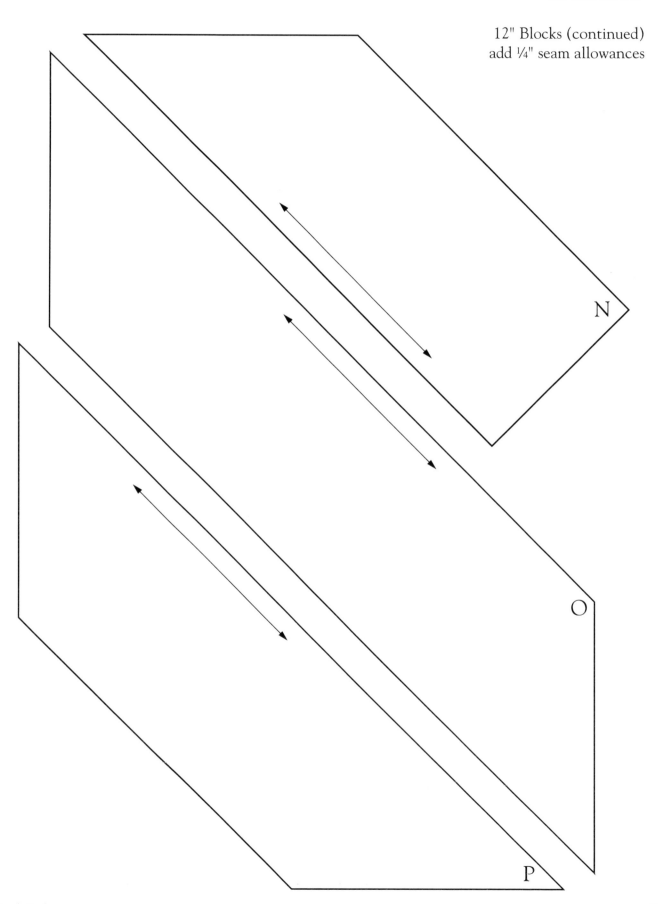

N

O

P

6-PATCH
BASKETS

12" Blocks (continued)
add ¼" seam allowances

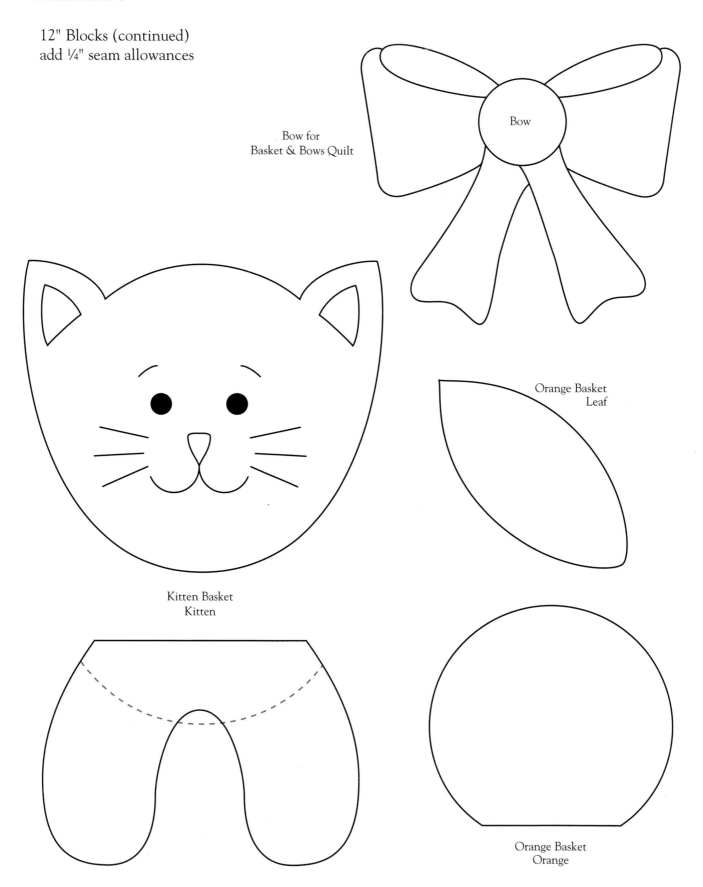

Bow for
Basket & Bows Quilt

Bow

Orange Basket
Leaf

Kitten Basket
Kitten

Orange Basket
Orange

SAWTOOTH BORDER WALL QUILT

Finished Size: 35" x 35"
12" Hanging Basket Block

This wall quilt, shown below, features four 12" Hanging Basket blocks framed by a complementary Sawtooth border. Instructions are given for using that block, but this border treatment would work nicely with a four-block setting of any 12" block.

YARDAGE

1½ yards green solid for blocks, pieced border, solid border, binding and optional tabs
¾ yards rust solid for blocks and pieced border
1¼ yards each backing fabric and batting

INSTRUCTIONS

1. Cut four borders from the green fabric, each 4" x 37". Cut four binding strips, each 2½" x 40". Cut all strips on the lengthwise grain.
2. Make four Hanging Basket blocks (or another 12" block). Sew them together into a four-block unit with the base of each basket at an outer corner.
3. Make 40 triangle-squares for the pieced border. Refer to the general instructions on page 13 for the quick-piecing technique. Each triangle-square has a finished size of 2" square. For traditional piecing,

use Triangle A given on page 56.
4. Join the triangle-square units into eight strips of five units each. Make four each of the two strips shown in Figure 1.

Figure 1

5. Make four joining triangle combinations as shown in Figure 2.
   Triangle W is given below.

Figure 2

6. Make four border strips by joining one triangle-square strip (Step 4) to either side of each Step 5 unit.
7. Sew a corner square onto two of the border strips. The corner is Pattern G, given on page 56.
8. Sew the two borders without corners onto opposite sides of the four-block unit, matching center seams. Sew the strips with corners onto remaining sides.
9. Add plain borders. See the general instructions on adding and mitering borders, quilting and binding. Full-size quilting patterns for the quilting design shown are offered on page 127.

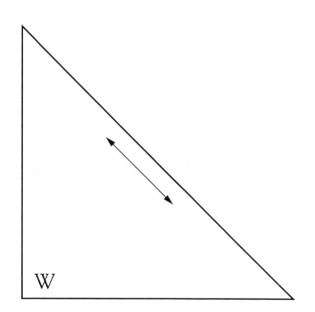

W

PARQUET BASKET BED QUILT

Finished Size: 74" x 91"
12" Parquet Basket Block

The quilt pictured on page 64 uses the 6-Patch Parquet Basket block. Instructions are given for using that block, but any 12" block can be used.

YARDAGE

2¾ yards Fabric #1 (stripe fabric) for setting triangles and basket patchwork
4 yards Fabric #2 (navy print) for borders and setting triangles
1½ yards Fabric #3 (medium blue print) for background of basket blocks
1 yard Fabric #4 (red print) for basket patchwork and binding
Optional: 1 yard Fabric #5 (navy solid) for basket handles and bases or cut from scraps of Fabric #2
6 yards backing fabric
Batting, larger than 74" x 91"

CUTTING INSTRUCTIONS

Always cut borders and binding strips from yardage before cutting smaller pieces for patchwork. Measurements given for cutting borders and binding are at least 2-3" longer than the exact length needed to allow for any discrepancies in piecing. Exact trimming can be done when borders are sewn onto the quilt top.

1. Make templates for the basket block of your choice. Refer to the general instructions and make a template for a half-block setting triangle for a 12" block; label the triangle Template Z. Make a template for a half-block setting triangle for a 6" block; label the triangle Template W. These patterns are finished size; add ¼" seam allowances before cutting fabric pieces.

2. On shelf paper or freezer paper, draw patterns for the X and Y borders as shown in Figures 1 and 2. The dimensions for these patterns do not include ¼" seam allowances. Cut out the paper patterns.

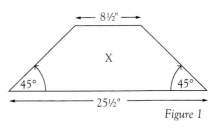

Figure 1

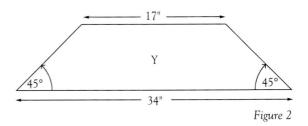

Figure 2

3. From Fabric #1 (stripe), cut eight strips, each 3" x 81", to make the Z setting triangles. Cut the strips consistently so all strips are identical; set aside. Cut eight identical triangles with Template W, placing the long side of the triangle along the stripe. Add ¼" seam allowances to W triangles before cutting from fabric. From the remainder, cut P pieces for 18 Parquet Basket blocks, positioning the template so the stripes are parallel to the grain line arrow, or cut pieces for the block of your choice.

4. From Fabric #2 (navy print), cut two 3½" x 94" border strips and two 3½" x 77" border strips for the outer borders. Cut four 4" x 81" strips for the Z setting triangles; set aside. Using the X and Y border patterns, cut two Y borders and four X borders.

5. From Fabric #3 (medium blue), cut background pieces for 18 blocks.

6. From Fabric #4 (red), cut eight 2½" wide strips across the fabric width for binding. From remainder, cut C triangles for 18 Parquet baskets or pieces for the block of your choice.

7. From Fabric #5 (navy solid) or from the remaining Fabric #2 scraps, cut basket handles and bases for 18 basket blocks.

MAKING THE Z SETTING TRIANGLES

1. Sew a strip set by sewing a Fabric #1 strip to both long sides of a Fabric #2 strip. Make four strip sets.

2. Refer to Figure 3 and use Template Z to cut seven setting triangles from each strip set (28 total). Add ¼" seam allowances to all triangles before cutting them from fabric.

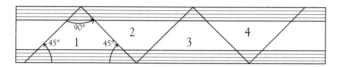

Figure 3

MAKING THE QUILT

1. Make 18 Parquet Basket blocks (or another 12" block of your choice). Refer to the general instructions, page 11, for tips on basket handles.

2. Refer to the quilt diagram and sew four baskets into a large square with the basket bases toward the center of the square.

3. Sew pairs of W triangles together to make four large triangles. Sew a large triangle to the short top edge of the X borders. Make two as shown in Figure 4 and two reverse. Sew the X borders to the quilt center.

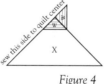

Figure 4

4. Sew the Y borders to the quilt center. Sew border corner seams.

5. Make the top and bottom borders by sewing together three blocks and six Z setting triangles as shown in Figure 5. Sew the borders to the quilt.

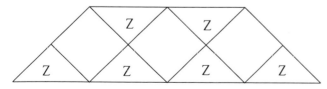

Figure 5

6. Make side borders in the same manner, using four blocks and eight Z setting triangles for each border. Sew borders to quilt sides. Sew border corner seams.

FINISHING THE QUILT

1. Sew the Fabric #2 borders to the quilt. Refer to the general instructions for tips on adding and mitering borders.

2. Quilt as desired.

3. After quilting, add binding as described in the general instructions.

Parquet Basket Bed Quilt

TINY BASKETS BED QUILT

Finished Size: 55¾" x 70⅛"
6" Tiny Baskets Block

The quilt shown below uses the Tiny Baskets block. Instructions are for that block, but you can substitute any 6" block in this setting, drafting your own patterns for a 3" border block, or eliminating it. This quilt is a coverlet for a double bed. It does not allow for a pillow tuck or drop at sides and end.

YARDAGE

3 yards Fabric #1 (rust solid) for plain blocks, setting triangles and borders
1½ yards Fabric #2 (muslin) for basket backgrounds
¾ yard Fabric #3 (dark brown solid) for binding
Assorted 6" squares for baskets and handles (the quilt pictured above used 133 different earth-tone prints)
4½ yards backing fabric
Pre-cut batting larger than 56" x 71" or equivalent yardage (4½ yards, 48" wide) for piecing the batting

CUTTING INSTRUCTIONS

1. Cut four 6⅞" x 58" borders and one 2⅝" x 58" border from Fabric #1. Borders will be trimmed to length when added to quilt top. Cut 20 alternate plain blocks, 6½" square. From the rest of Fabric #1, cut 18 half-block triangles and four quarter-block triangles. (See general instructions on diagonal sets). For the pillow border, cut six 5½" squares. Divide the squares diagonally both ways to make 24 Y triangles. Cut two 3" squares; divide each square diagonally one way to make two Z triangles per square.

2. For binding, cut seven strips on the crosswise grain, each 2½" x 45", and the diagram on page 66.

3. From remaining fabrics, cut the appropriate pieces for 30 Tiny Basket blocks or another 6" basket block of your choice. For the pillow border, cut pieces for thirteen 3" baskets. Cut handles for all baskets. (See the general instructions on making bias handles.)

QUILT INSTRUCTIONS

1. Make thirty 6" basket blocks, plus thirteen 3" single baskets for the pillow border.
2. Set basket blocks together with plain squares and setting triangles. Refer to the general instructions on diagonal sets, and the diagram on page 66.
3. Trim border strips to size, then sew them to the sides and bottom of the assembled quilt top.
4. Assemble the pillow border strip as shown. Sew the narrow border to the bottom of the assembled strip and the wide border to the top of it. Then, sew the completed pillow border to the top of the quilt.
5. To complete the quilt, follow the general instructions for quilting and binding.

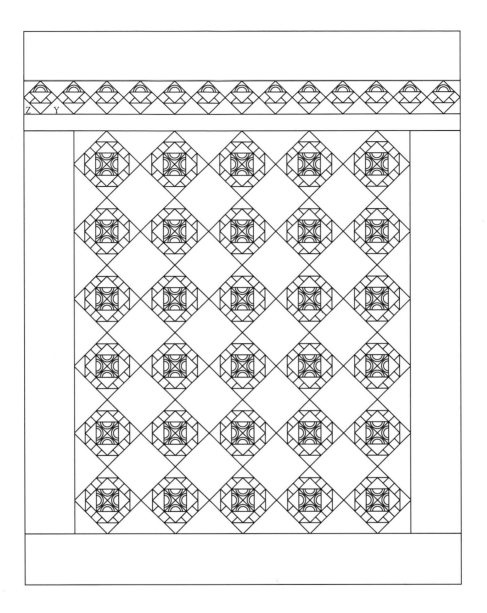

Tiny Basket Bed Quilt

Mini Basket Wall Quilt

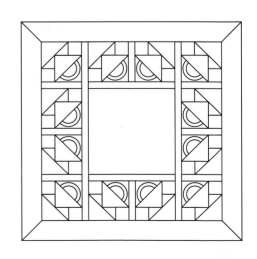

MINI-BASKETS WALL QUILT

Finished Size: 16½" x 16½"
6" Tiny Baskets Block

This small quilt, pictured below, uses quarter-block sections (3" finished single baskets) of the 6-Patch Tiny Baskets pattern. Twelve different scrap fabrics were used in the quilt pictured below, but the design could also be made with twelve baskets which are alike.

YARDAGE

½ yard Fabric #1 (muslin or cream solid) for center square and background of blocks

½ yard Fabric #2 (green print) for border, sashing and binding

Scraps (at least 5" x 5") of 12 different fabrics for baskets, or ⅓ yard of fabric to make the baskets all alike

⅓ yard backing fabric

Batting, larger than 16½" x 16½"

CUTTING INSTRUCTIONS

Always cut borders and binding strips from yardage before cutting pieces for patchwork or setting blocks. Measurements given for cutting borders and binding are longer than should be needed to allow for discrepancies in piecing. Exact trimming is done when borders are sewn to quilt top.

1. From Fabric #1 (muslin or cream solid), cut one 7" square for the center of the quilt.
2. From Fabric #2 (green print), cut two 2½" wide binding strips across the fabric width. Cut four 2" x 19" border strips, two 1" x 14" sashing strips, two 1" x 7" sashing strips and eight 1" x 3½" sashing strips.
3. From the remaining fabrics, cut the appropriate pieces for 12 baskets. Each basket is one-quarter of the Tiny Baskets block and will finish 3" square. Cut narrow bias strips for the handles as described in the general instructions.

QUILT INSTRUCTIONS

1. Make 12 quarter-block sections (3" finished baskets) of the 6" Tiny Baskets pattern. See general instructions, page 11, for information on making appliqué handles.
2. Referring to the quilt diagram on page 66, lay out the blocks and sashing strips around the center square.
3. Piece the quilt in three vertical rows, a wide center row with narrower rows to each side. To make the center row, sew a sashing strip to the top and bottom of the center square. Sew together the top two baskets, placing a short sashing strip between them; repeat for the bottom two baskets. Stitch the two-basket units to the sashing at the top and bottom of the center square. Sew a 1" x 14" sashing strip to opposite sides of the center row.
4. To make each side row, join four baskets, placing short sashing strips between the blocks. Sew the side rows to opposite sides of the center row.
5. Add border strips, mitering border corners. Refer to the general instructions for information on adding and mitering borders.
6. Follow the general instructions for quilting and binding. The quilt shown above is quilted in the ditch around the baskets and sashing strips, has diagonal rows of quilting in the border and a fancy quilting design in the center square.

TWELVE-BASKET CRADLE QUILT

Finished Size: 31½" x 40"
6" Kitten Basket Block

The quilt pictured on page 52 features the Kitten Basket block. Instructions are given for using that block, but any 6" block can be used.

YARDAGE

1¾ yards Fabric #1 (dark blue print) for border, binding, basket blocks and setting block frames
¾ yard Fabric #2 (solid cream or muslin) for block background and setting blocks
⅛ yard Fabric #3 (cream/blue print) for baskets
⅛ yard each (or scraps) of brown, tan, rust and gold pin-dot fabrics for kittens
1½ yards backing fabric.
Pre-cut batting larger than 31½" x 40" or equivalent yardage (1½ yards, 48" wide) for piecing the batting
Embroidery floss for kitten faces

CUTTING INSTRUCTIONS

Make templates for Patterns A, C, E, F, N and O, and the kitten, which are included in the 6" Block Patterns on pages 54-55.

Always cut borders and binding strips from yardage before cutting pieces for patchwork or setting blocks. Measurements given for cutting borders and binding are 2-3" longer than the exact length that should be needed to allow for discrepancies in piecing. Exact trimming is done when borders are sewn onto the quilt top.

1. From Fabric #1, cut the following:
   2 border strips 3½" x 43"
   2 border strips 3½" x 35"
   3 binding strips 2½" x 63"
   16 setting strips 1½" x 6½"
   10 setting strips 1½" x 6¾"
   10 setting strips 1½" x 5¾"
   12 setting strips 1½" x 4½".
   Cut borders and binding on the lengthwise grain.
2. Cut setting pieces from Fabric #2. Quick cut six 4½" squares for the setting squares. Cut three 7" squares and divide the squares in half diagonally both ways to make 12 half-block triangles (discard two). Cut two 3⅜" squares; divide the squares in half diagonally one way to make the four corner triangles.

3. From remaining fabrics, cut the appropriate pieces for 12 Kitten Basket blocks.

QUILT INSTRUCTIONS

1. Make 12 Kitten Basket blocks (or another 6" basket of your choice). See general instructions (page 10) for information on appliqué and making appliquéd handles. Appliqué kittens by hand, sewing paws on first and overlapping the head piece. Embroider face details.
2. Add stripping to setting blocks. First, sew all the 1½" x 4½" strips to opposite sides of the plain setting blocks. Then, sew 6½" strips to the remaining sides as shown in Figure 1.

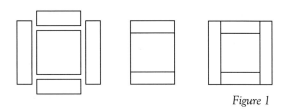

Figure 1

3. Add a 6½" long strip to the hypotenuse edge of each of the four corner triangles, as shown in Figure 2. Trim ends of strip even with the triangle sides.
4. Make 10 half-blocks. First, add a 1½" x 5¾" strip to one side of the triangle. Then, sew a 6¾" long strip at the top as shown in Figure 3. Trim strip ends to match the angle of the triangle.

Figure 2

Figure 3

5. Set basket blocks together with setting blocks, half-blocks and quarter-blocks as shown. See general instructions on diagonal sets (page 17).
6. Add border strips. Refer to general instructions for information on adding and mitering borders.
7. Follow general instructions for quilting and binding. The quilt shown on page 52 features a border quilting design that emphasizes the zigzag of the piecing. The plain blocks are quilted with a pretty basket grid. Quilting design is optional.

BASKET & BOWS QUILT

Finished Size: 75" x 92"
12" New York Basket Block

The quilt pictured on page 70 features New York Basket blocks with a bow added. Instructions are given for using this block, but any 12" block can be used. This quilt fits a standard 54" x 75" (double) mattress with a 6½" pillow tuck and a 10½" drop at the sides.

YARDAGE

4 yards Fabric #1 (blue/cream print) for basket blocks, middle border

2 yards Fabric #2 (muslin) for setting squares and triangles

2¾ yards Fabric #3 (slate blue print) for baskets, outer border

2¼ yards Fabric #4 (mauve print) for bows, inner border and binding

½ yard Fabric #5 (slate blue print) for basket patchwork

½ yard slate solid for basket handles

¼ yard plum solid for bows

5¼ yards backing fabric

Pre-cut batting larger than 75" x 92" or the equivalent yardage (5¼ yards, 48" wide) for piecing the batting

CUTTING INSTRUCTIONS

Always cut borders and binding first. Measurements given for cutting borders and binding are 2-3" longer than exact length needed to allow for discrepancies in piecing. Exact trimming can be done when borders are sewn onto the quilt top. Cut borders and binding on lengthwise grain.

1. Cut borders and binding:
   Fabric #1 – Two strips 6½" x 88" and two strips 6½" x 70".
   Fabric #3 – Two strips 4½" x 96" and two strips 4½" x 78".
   Fabric #4 – Two strips 2½" x 75" and two strips 2½" x 58" for borders; five binding strips 2½" x 71".

2. From Fabric #2, cut six setting squares, 10 half-block triangles and four quarter-block corner triangles. See the general instructions on diagonal sets.

3. From the remaining fabric, cut the appropriate pieces for 12 New York Basket blocks and 12 bows. The pattern for the appliqué bow is on page 60.

MAKING THE QUILT

1. Make 12 New York Basket blocks.

2. Set basket blocks together with setting blocks and triangles as shown in the diagram above left. Finished size of the quilt top should now be approximately 51½" x 68½".

3. Refer to the general instructions (page 18) for tips on adding and mitering borders, quilting and binding. Quilting design is optional. The quilt shown features a feather/heart design in the plain blocks and middle border. This full-size design is on page 82.

This double bed-sized Basket & Bows Quilt features an alternate setting of New York Basket Blocks. The bow like that in the Bow-Knot Basket adds just the right touch. Instructions begin on page 69.

UPRIGHT
BASKETS

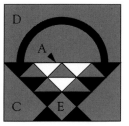

Woman's Basket

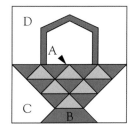

Colonial Basket

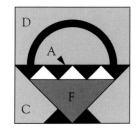

Iowa Basket

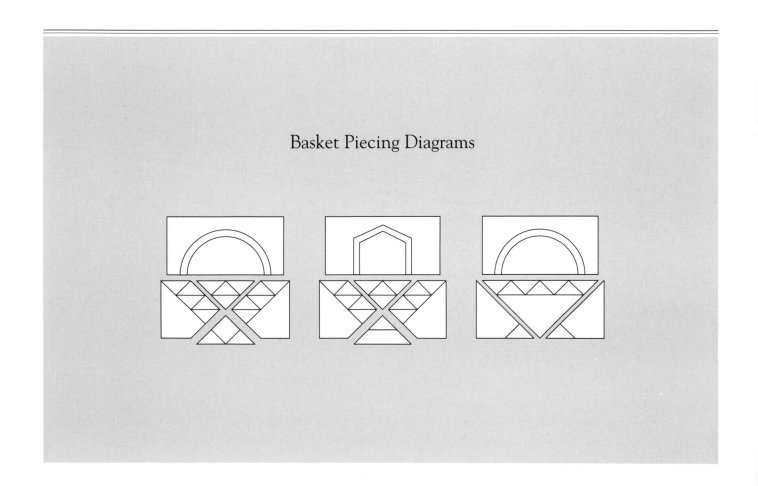

Basket Piecing Diagrams

6" Blocks
add ¼" seam allowances

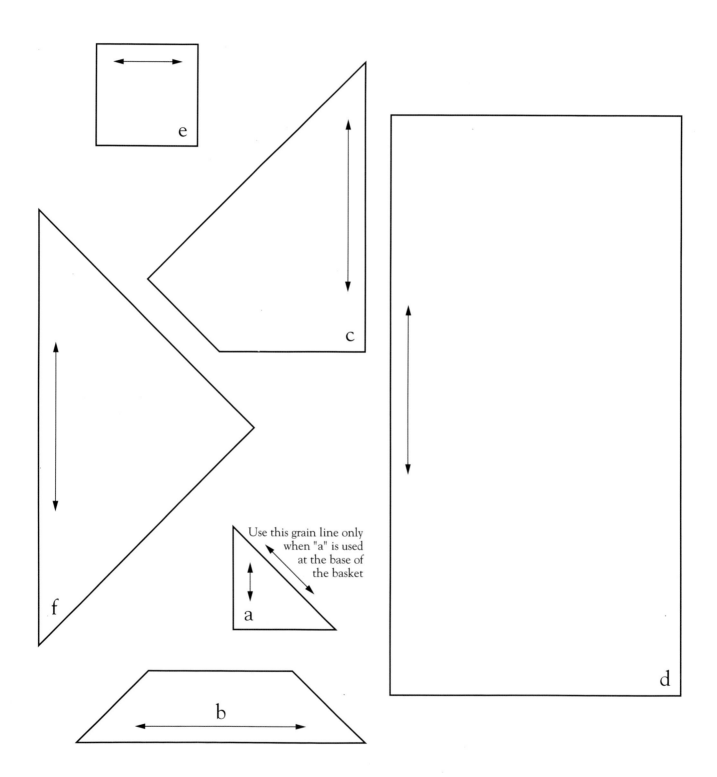

Use this grain line only
when "a" is used
at the base of
the basket

a

e

c

d

f

b

12" Blocks
add ¼" seam allowances

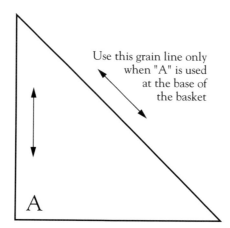

Use this grain line only
when "A" is used
at the base of
the basket

A

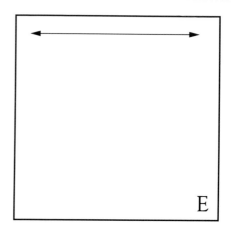

E

center line ▲

D

12" Blocks (continued)
add ¼" seam allowances

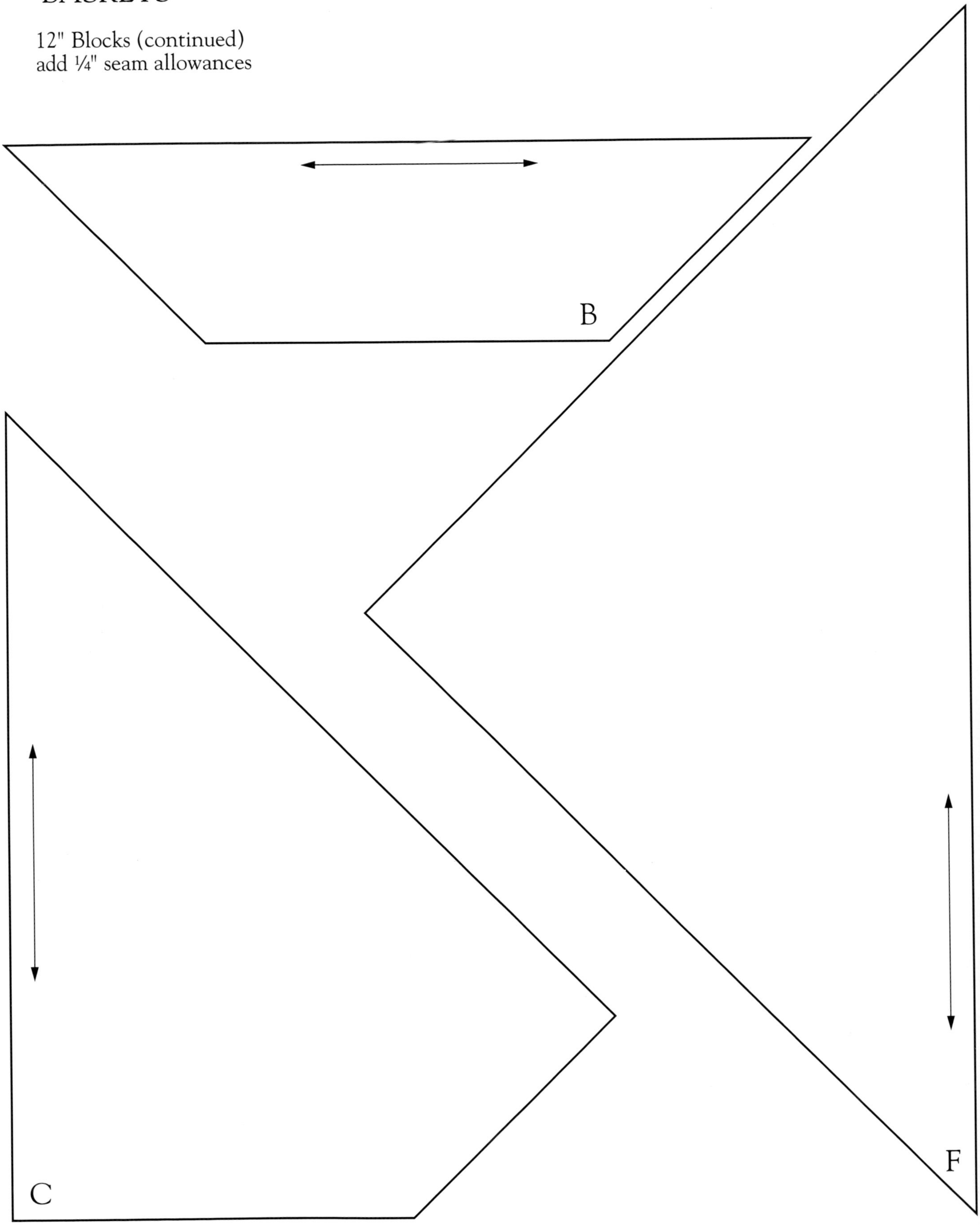

B

C

F

BASKET POCKET TOTE BAG

Finished Size: 12" x 14" x 3" or 6" x 7" x 1½"
Any 12" or 6" Upright Basket Block

The tote bags shown on page 21 feature an assortment of Upright Basket blocks. These instructions are for use with any of the Upright Basket blocks. Yardage and measurements are given for 12" blocks with figures for 6" blocks stated in parentheses. Seam allowances (¼" throughout) are included in figures for cut pieces. The tote is made so that the lower half of the basket block forms a lined pocket on each side of the bag and the bag handles create the look of basket handles (no D piece is used).

YARDAGE

¾ yard (½ yard) heavy fabric for bag, such as denim, poplin or duck

1 yard (½ yard) broadcloth-weight fabric for basket patchwork, bag lining and handle contrast

¼ yard or scraps of coordinating fabric for additional basket patchwork

CUTTING INSTRUCTIONS

1. Cut the following pieces from the heavy bag fabric. Remember that ¼" seam allowances are already included in the measurements stated.
    Two handles 2" x 30" (1½" x 18")
    Two bag fronts 12½" x 15" (6½" x 8")
    Two bottom pocket strips 2" x 12½" (1½" x 6½")
    Side and bottom inset 3½" x 43" (2" x 22½")

2. Cut the following pieces from the lining fabric:
    Two handles 1½" x 30" (1" x 18)
    Two bag fronts 12½" x 15" (6½" x 8")
    Side and bottom inset 3½" x 42" (2" x 22)
    Two pocket linings 8" x 12½" (4½" x 6½")

3. Use the remaining fabric to cut pieces for the basket patchwork. Do not cut a Pattern D piece.

SEWING INSTRUCTIONS

1. Make two baskets, eliminating the Pattern D piece.

2. Sew a bottom pocket strip to the bottom edge of each sewn basket.

3. Place one pocket together with one pocket lining, matching right sides and all edges. Sew them together at the top edge with a ¼" seam. Repeat with the other pocket. Press linings over to wrong side of pocket.

4. Position a pocket at the bottom of each bag front, matching raw edges at bottom and sides. Baste pockets in place on all three sides.

5. Right sides together, sew side/bottom inset piece to one bag piece, sewing down one side, across the bottom and up the remaining side in one continuous seam, pivoting at corners. Reinforce corners, as this is usually the point of stress when the bag is used. Sew the remaining bag front to the opposite side of the inset in the same way. Trim inset even with top of bag. You may find it necessary to clip seam allowances at the corners.

6. Make a bag lining in the same manner, sewing one lining piece to either side of the lining inset strip. Leave an opening in the center of one bottom seam to turn the bag right side out later. Trim ½" from the top raw edge around the completed bag lining.

7. Slip lining inside bag, placing right sides together. Align the top edges and sew all around the top edge. Turn bag right side out through opening in lining. Hand stitch the opening closed.

8. Push lining down into bag so that bag and lining bottoms meet. The top edge of the bag fabric will fold over to the inside of the bag (¼" to ⅜"). Press top edge, then topstitch ¼" from the edge around the bag.

9. Pin handle and handle lining right sides together. The bag fabric strip is wider than the lining piece so that it creates a piped look when the handle is turned right side out. See photo on page 21. Sew the handle pieces together along both long edges. Be sure raw edges are together as you sew each long edge. Turn handle right side out through one end and press. Topstitch close to the folds.

10. Position ends of handles on the bag below the top edge of each pocket. Machine stitch the handle bottoms to the bag, sewing through the bag and lining. Repeat this top stitching (sewing through handles, bag and lining) approximately 1" below the top edge of the bag.

Twelve-Basket Quilt with Pieced Border

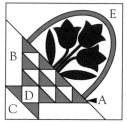

Cathy's Tulip Basket

Bow-Knot Basket

Basket of Flowers

Basket Piecing Diagrams

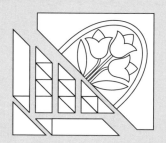

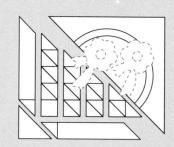

6" Blocks
add ¼" seam allowances

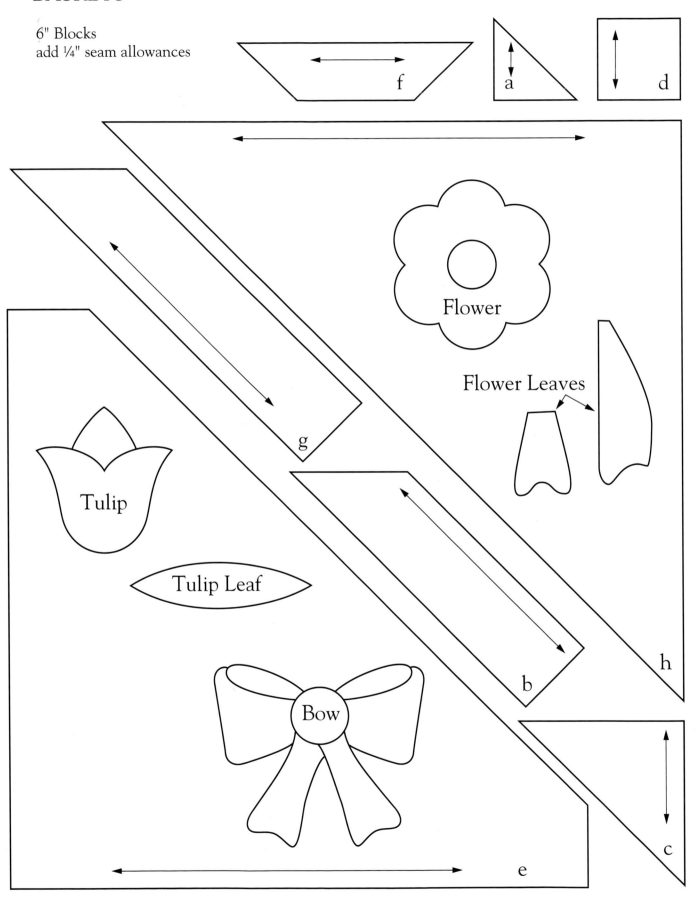

f

a

d

Flower

Flower Leaves

g

Tulip

Tulip Leaf

b

h

Bow

c

e

12" Blocks
add ¼" seam allowances

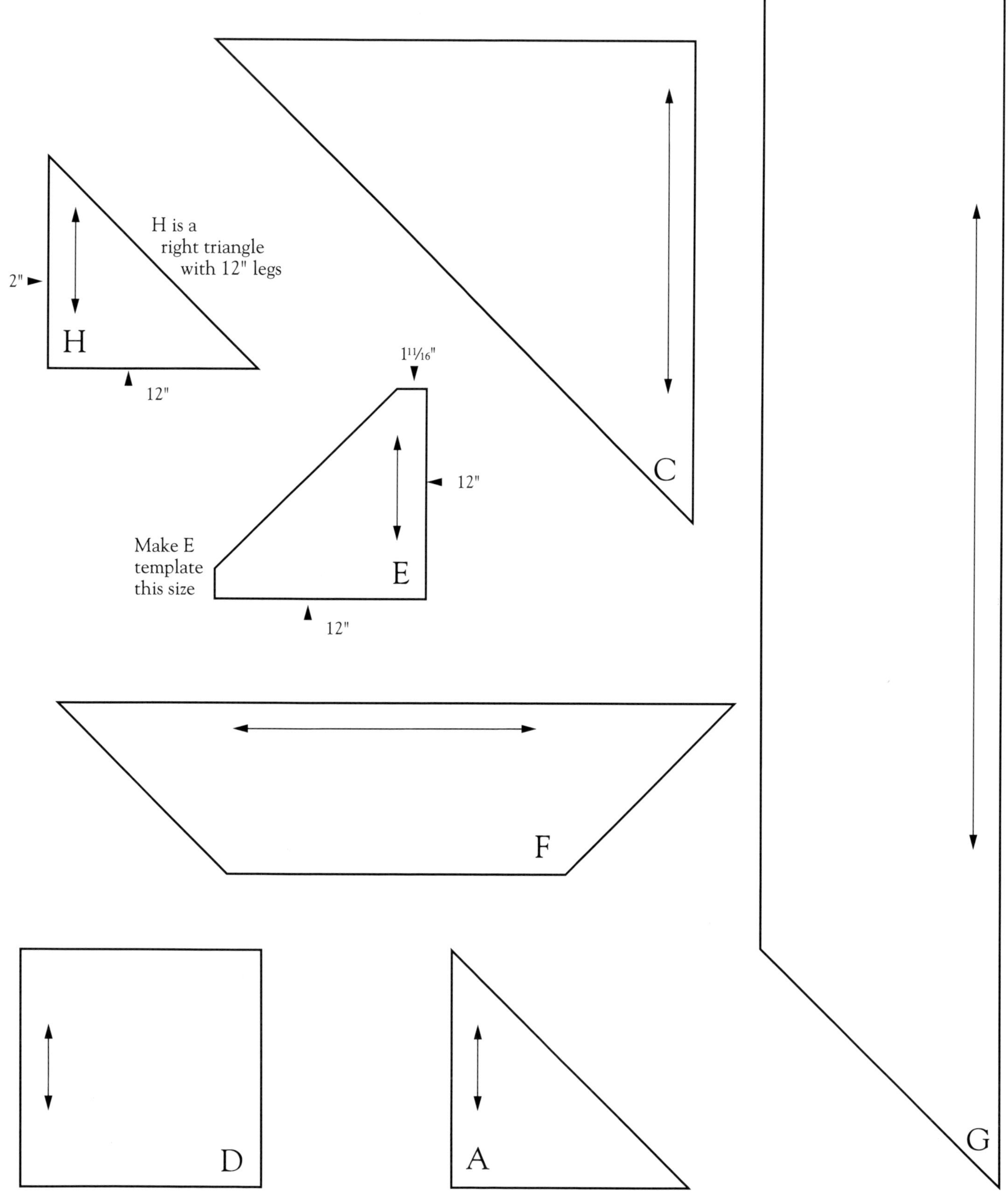

H is a
right triangle
with 12" legs

2" ▶

H

12"

C

1¹¹⁄₁₆"

12"

Make E
template
this size

E

12"

F

D

A

G

12" Blocks (continued)
add ¼" seam allowances

Tulip Leaf

Tulip

Flower

Flower Leaf

B

Flower Leaf

Bow

ONE-BASKET WALL QUILT

Finished Size: 29" x 29"
12" Basket of Flowers Block

The wallhanging shown below features the Basket of Flowers block. Instructions are given for using that block, but any 12" block can be used. The same wallhanging made using the 7-Patch Cactus Basket block is shown bottom, right.

YARDAGE (for wallhanging shown above)

¾ yards Fabric #1 (light blue) for corner triangles, block background, binding and hanging tabs

½ yard Fabric #2 (dark blue print) for basket patchwork and outer border

¼ yard Fabric #3 (cream solid) for basket patchwork

¼ yard each (or scrap) of burgundy, pink and dark green prints and a pink solid for flowers and leaves

⅜ yard fabric for inner border, basket frame
(Note: If using stripe as shown, you will need ¾ yard to cut stripe on the lengthwise grain)

1 yard each of backing fabric and batting

CUTTING INSTRUCTIONS

1. From Fabric #1, cut four binding strips 2½" x 32". To cut corner triangles, cut two 10⅞" squares. Divide each square in half diagonally to make a total of four triangles that include seam allowances.

2. Cut four border strips from Fabric #2, 3½" x 32".

3. For the inner border, cut four strips 2" x 24". For the basket frame, cut four strips 1½" x 15".

4. From the remaining fabric, cut the appropriate pieces for the basket block and hanging tabs. See the general instructions for tabs on page 20.

QUILT INSTRUCTIONS

1. Make any 12" basket block of your choice.

2. Stitch the framing strips to all sides of the block. See the general instructions on mitering corners.

3. Add corner triangles as shown. Handle triangles carefully to avoid stretching the bias edge.

4. Add inner and outer borders as shown. See the general instructions on mitering corners.

5. A full-size quilting pattern for the corner triangles (used in the quilts shown) is given on page 82. Quilting design is optional.

6. Finish the quilt with binding and hanging tabs as desired. Refer to the general instructions.

Cactus Basket Wall Quilt

Twelve-Basket Quilt With Pieced Border

One-Basket Quilting Pattern

TWELVE-BASKET QUILT WITH PIECED BORDER

Finished Size: 73½" x 90½"
12" Cathy's Tulip Basket Block

The quilt shown on page 76 uses Cathy's Tulip Basket block and instructions are given for using that block. You can use any 12" block. The quilt shown was designed by Cathy Bruett.

YARDAGE

3½ yards Fabric #1 (cream solid) for background of basket blocks, setting blocks and triangles, squares in pieced border

2¾ yards Fabric #2 (dark green solid) for outer border, appliquéd leaves and stems

2¼ yards Fabric #3 (light rust) for inner border and appliqué flowers

3 yards Fabric #4 (dark brown print) for baskets, handles, border triangles and binding

¼ yard (dark rust) fabric for flowers

5½ yards backing fabric

Batting, larger than 73½" x 90½"

CUTTING INSTRUCTIONS

Always cut borders and binding strips from yardage before cutting pieces for patchwork or setting blocks. Measurements given for cutting borders and binding are 2"-3" longer than the exact measurement needed. Exact trimming is done when borders are sewn to quilt top.

1. From Fabric #1, cut six plain squares, ten half-block triangles and four quarter-block triangles. Refer to the general instructions on cutting setting squares and triangles. This fabric is also used for the squares in the pieced border. Cut fifty 4½" squares with rotary cutter.
2. From Fabric #2, cut two outer border strips 3⁵⁄₁₆" x 94" and two strips 3⁵⁄₁₆" x 77".
3. From Fabric #3, cut two inner border strips 3⁵⁄₁₆" x 78" and two strips 3⁵⁄₁₆" x 60".
4. Cut four binding strips from Fabric #4, each 2½" x 90". Cut on the lengthwise grain.

5. To cut the 92 S border triangles, use rotary cutter to cut twenty-three 7" squares from Fabric #4. Divide the squares diagonally both ways to produce the needed triangles. To cut the 16 T corner triangles, cut eight squares, 3¾" x 3¾". Cut the squares in half diagonally into two triangles per square.
6. Use the remaining fabrics to cut the appropriate pieces for 12 basket blocks.

QUILT INSTRUCTIONS

1. Make 12 Cathy's Tulip Basket blocks or another 12" block of your choice. Refer to general instructions on appliqué and curved handles.
2. Set the basket blocks together with plain squares and setting triangles as shown. Refer to the general instructions on diagonal sets.
3. Add the inner border. Refer to the general instructions on adding and mitering borders.
4. Construct the pieced border by making top and bottom strips and two side strips.
5. Add pieced borders to sides of quilt top, then the top and bottom edges.
6. Add outer border.
7. To finish the quilt, refer to the general instructions for tips on quilting and binding.

Instructions for the Basket of Lilies Wall Quilt begin on page 90.

DIAMOND
BASKETS

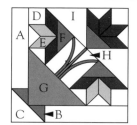

Basket of Lilies

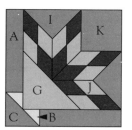

Diamond Tulip Basket

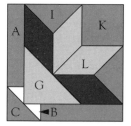

Cactus Basket

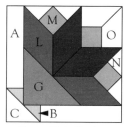

State Fair Basket

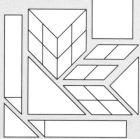

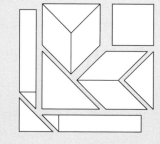

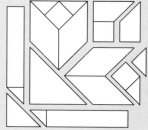

Basket Piecing Diagrams

6" Blocks
add ¼" seam allowances

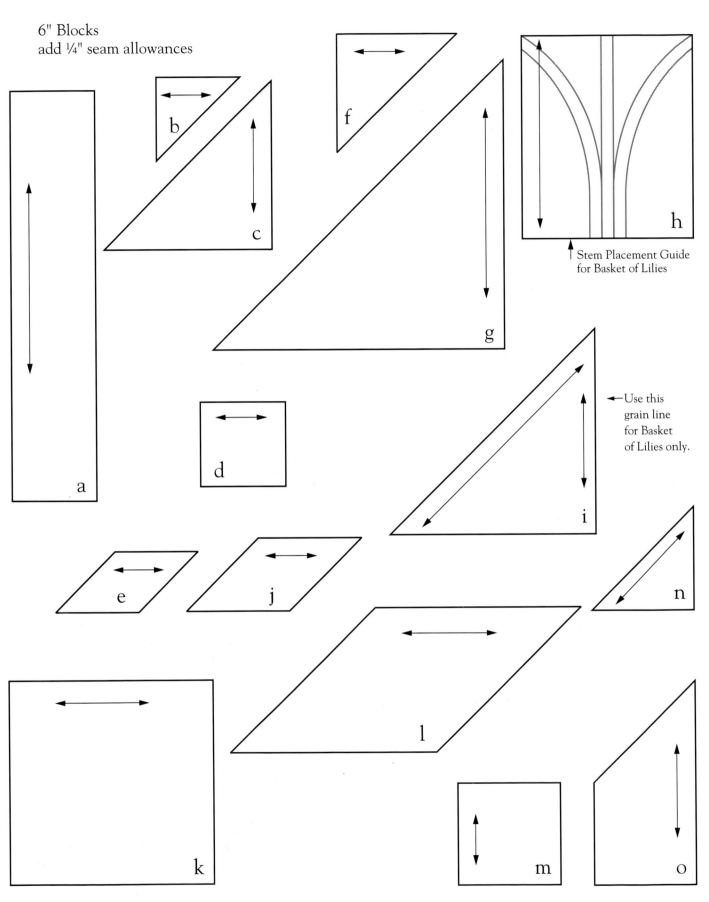

Stem Placement Guide
for Basket of Lilies

Use this
grain line
for Basket
of Lilies only.

12" Blocks
add ¼" seam allowances

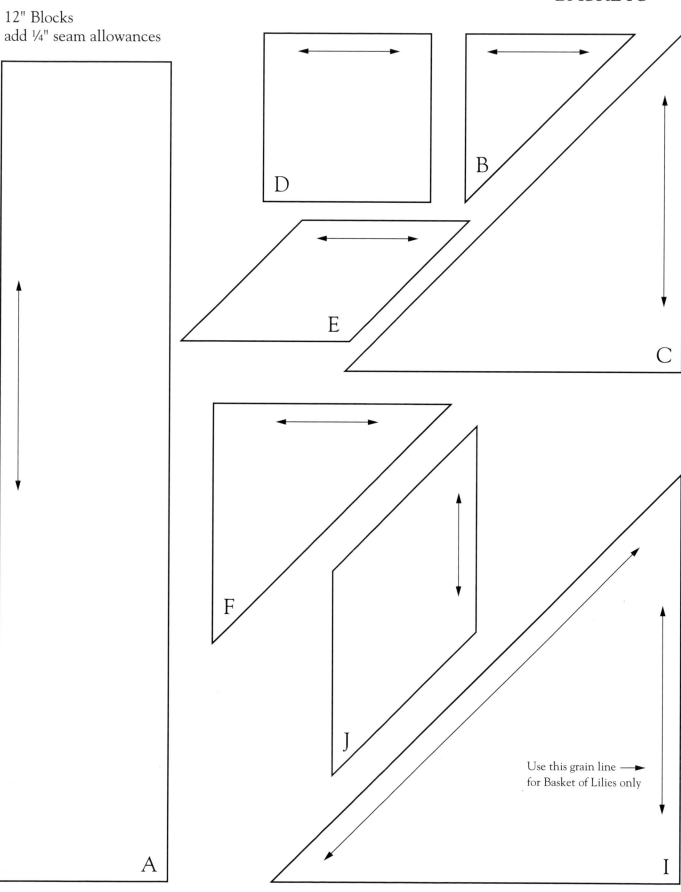

A

B

C

D

E

F

I

J

Use this grain line →
for Basket of Lilies only

DIAMOND
BASKETS

12" Blocks (continued)
add ¼" seam allowances

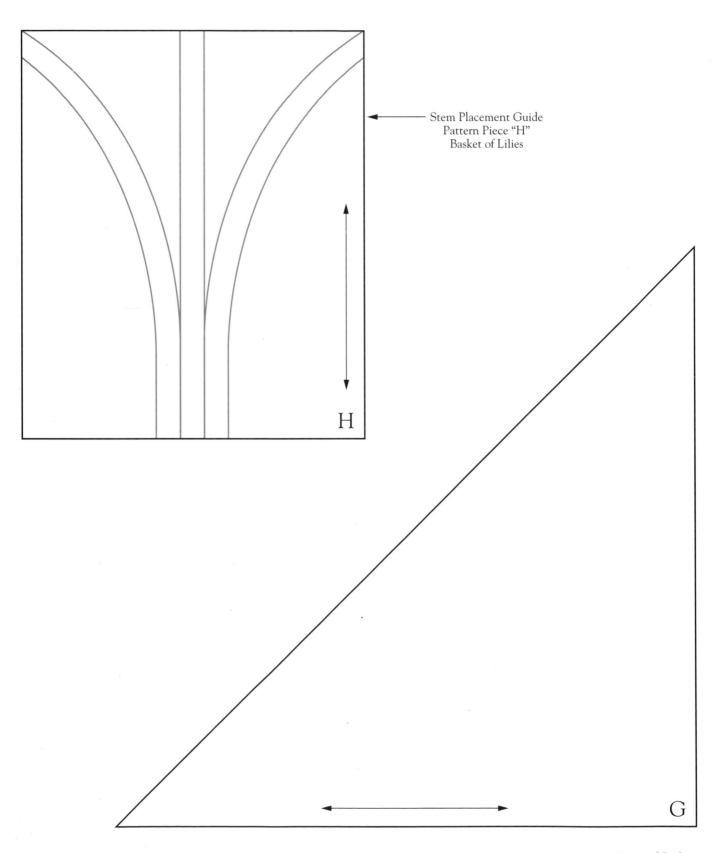

Stem Placement Guide
Pattern Piece "H"
Basket of Lilies

H

G

12" Blocks (continued)
add ¼" seam allowances

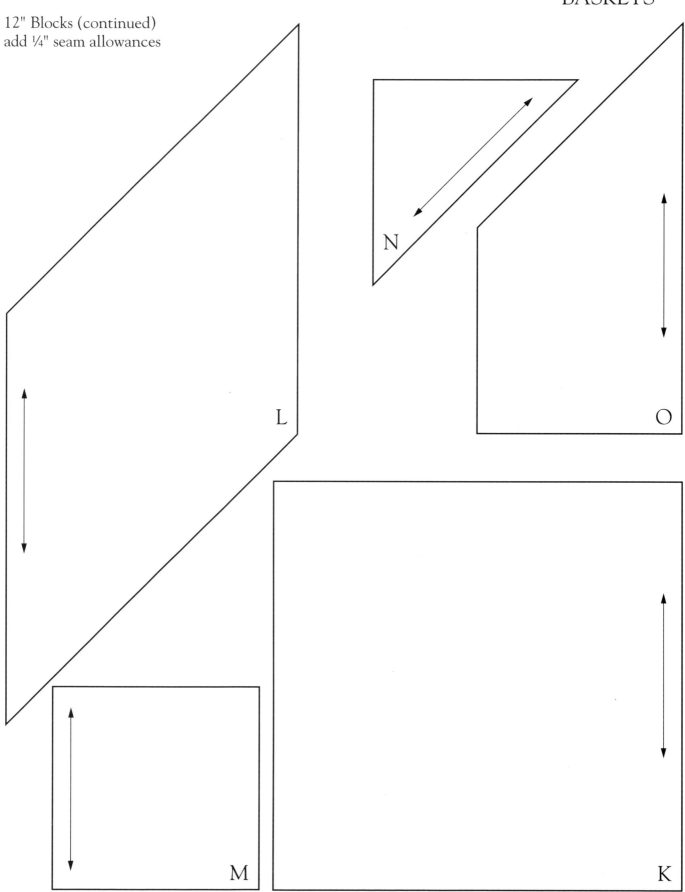

N

L

O

M

K

BASKET OF LILIES WALL QUILT

Finished Size: 21" x 27"
12" Basket of Lilies Block

The wallhanging shown on page 84 uses the Basket of Lilies block. Instructions are given for using that block, but any 12" block can be used.

YARDAGE

1 yard Fabric #1 (lengthwise stripes) for borders and Pattern X

¾ yard Fabric #2 (plum solid) for basket and Patterns Y and Z

¼ yard Fabric #3 (mauve solid) for background of basket block

¼ yard or scraps of three prints (one lavender, two navy) for flowers and one (light green) for stems

1 yard each of backing fabric and batting

CUTTING INSTRUCTIONS

1. Cut two border strips from Fabric #1, 2½" x 30", and two strips 2½" x 24". Cut borders lengthwise, following the stripe consistently so that, when corners are mitered, the stripes will match. Borders are cut slightly longer than needed to allow for discrepancies – exact trimming will be done when borders are sewn onto the quilt top and mitered.

2. From Fabric #2, cut three strips 2½" x 45" for binding, cutting on the crosswise grain.

3. Make templates of the three special patterns given on page 91. Cut eight of Triangle X from Fabric #1. Place the hypotenuse of the triangle consistently along the stripe. From Fabric #2, cut four of Pattern Y and two of Pattern Z.

4. From remaining fabrics, cut the appropriate pieces for one 12" Basket of Lilies block. Use the same patterns B, D and E to cut the appropriate pieces for the corner flowers as shown in the diagram.

QUILT INSTRUCTIONS

1. Make one 12" Basket of Lilies block.

2. Sew pairs of Triangle X together to make four larger triangles. Sew these to each side of the basket block at top and bottom as shown.

3. For the corner flowers, sew border diamonds into groups of three with B triangles inset as shown in Figure 1. Make four "right" units and four "left" units.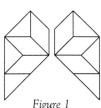

Figure 1

4. Lay all units out on a flat surface, in position. Match and sew each of the three-diamond corners to an adjacent Y or Z trapezoid.

5. Sew border sections with Z trapezoids to the top and bottom of the center basket unit. Sew remaining border units onto the sides of the piece as shown. Where borders meet, make a seam to join diamonds at corners.

6. Set in D squares at corners.

7. Add striped border. To finish the wall quilt, refer to general instructions on quilting and binding.

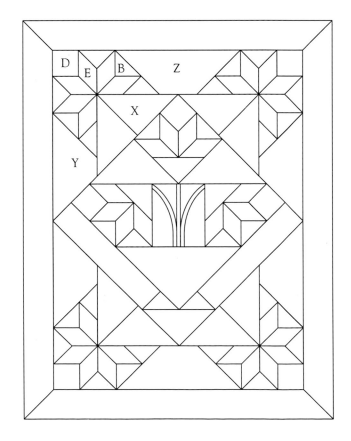

Special Patterns for Basket of Lilies Wall Quilt
add ¼" seam allowance

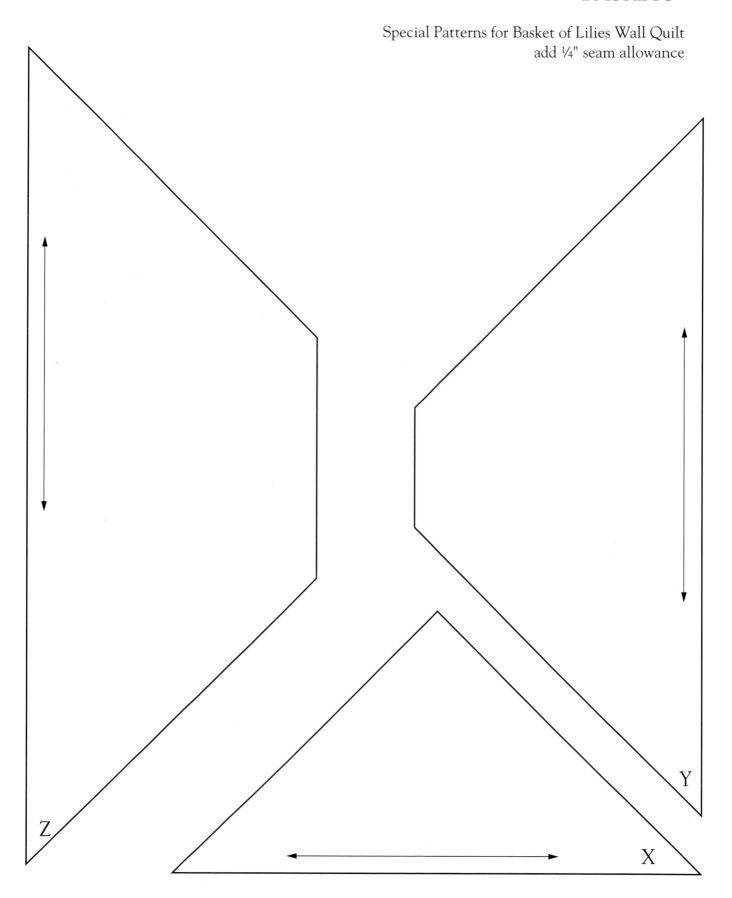

PADDED FRAMES

Finished Size: 11" or 17" Square
Any 6" or 12" Basket block

These instructions are for use with any 6" or 12" basket block. Yardage and measurements are given for 12" blocks with figures for 6" blocks in parentheses.

SUPPLIES & YARDAGE

Four wooden stretcher strips 17" (11") long
Staple gun and ¼" staples
Fabric scraps for patchwork block
¾ yard (½ yard) fabric for wide border
½ yard (¼ yard) fabric for narrow stripe border
24" (18") square of backing fabric
24" (18") square of regular quilt batting
¼ yard of extra-thick (1") batting

INSTRUCTIONS

1. Cut four narrow border strips 1" x 18" (1" x 9"). Cut four wide border strips 5½" x 24" (5½" x 18"). Sew borders onto the completed patchwork block. Refer to the general instructions on mitering borders.

2. Layer the patchwork, the regular batting and backing fabric. Quilt as desired. Quilt the outer edge of the basket block and "in the ditch" around the outer edge of the narrow border.

3. Assemble stretcher strips to make a frame. Lay the quilted block face down and center the frame on the wrong side. Stretch the backing fabric back tightly over the frame (push pins are good for holding fabric in place while you center the block). When the block is correctly centered over the frame, staple the backing fabric just inside the outer edge of the frame. Trim excess backing close to staples.

4. Turn the project right side up. Fold the wide border fabric and batting into the center to keep them out of the way as you work. Cut strips of the thick batting big enough to just cover the flat part of the frame. (These can be lightly glued in place, if desired.)  Smooth batting over the added thick strips; trim all layers of batting even with the outer edge of the frame.

5. Smooth wide border over batting. Carefully turn the frame over so that wrong side is up. Pull the border fabric over the padded stretcher strips to the wrong side of the frame, folding under the raw edge of the fabric. Hold edges in place with push pins. Check the front repeatedly as you work to be sure the fabric is pulled smooth and taut without puckers.

6. Begin stapling in the center of each strip, working out toward the ends. Stop stapling about 1" from the corners.

7. To eliminate extra fabric, trim off a 3" triangle of the border fabric at the corners. Match the mitered seam of the border with the mitered joining of the frame and put a staple in the center, straddling the seam. Make a small pleat by rolling in the excess fabric about ½" on either side of the corner and staple the pleat to the frame. The pleats may be pressed with an iron to flatten them when stapling is completed.

PATCHWORK ALBUM COVERS

Finished Size: Varies
Any 3", 6" or 12" Block

The photo on page 21 shows that both diagonal and upright basket blocks can be used to make unique fabric covers. For this project, the purchased album or notebook must have front and back covers that bend back to allow the fabric cover to be slipped on.

YARDAGE

Yardage will vary depending on the size of the notebook you wish to cover. For a standard three-ring binder, you will need ½ yard of a cover fabric, plus coordinating fabric scraps for the basket patchwork. The project also calls for an equal amount of thin batting.

INSTRUCTIONS

1. Make a basket block of your choice, 3", 6" or 12" square, to decorate the front of the album.
2. Measure the front of the notebook. If the notebook or album is padded, use a tape measure instead of a ruler to measure. Add triangles and/or fabric strips to the prepared basket block to create a piece the same size as the album front plus ½" seam allowances on all sides. It is wise to sketch your patchwork plan on graph paper before cutting fabric.
3. Prepare front cover facing, back & back cover facing. The size of the front cover facing is identical to the prepared front cover. The back and back cover facing consist of a single, continuous rectangle – its height is the

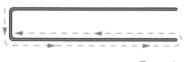

Figure 1

same as the prepared block. To determine its length, use a measuring tape to measure as shown in Figure 1. Do not measure the album opened out flat.

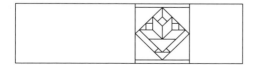

Figure 2

4. Using ½" seam allowances, sew the front cover facing and the back/back cover facing unit to either side of the prepared front cover as shown in Figure 2.
5. Cut a piece of batting the exact height of the album. The length of the batting piece should be 1" shorter than the prepared fabric cover. Center this piece of batting on the wrong side of the fabric cover and pin it in place. There should be ½" of fabric extending beyond the batting on all sides.
6. Fold ½" of fabric over the batting at both sides and stitch down, sewing ¼" from the edge of the fabric. Leave the top and bottom edges alone for now.
7. Turn the cover over so the right side of the fabric is up. Fold both front and back facing sections toward the center, right sides of fabric together. Be sure that the front fold is the front edge seam and the back fold coin-

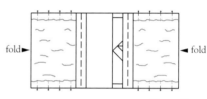

Figure 3

cides with the back edge of the album. You might want to trial fit the album at this point. When satisfied that the positioning is correct, pin facings in place at top and bottom edges as shown in Figure 3.
8. Cut two fabric strips for the album spine facing. These should be 1" wide and long enough to overlap the cover facings by 1", as shown in Figure 4. With the right side down, pin each of these

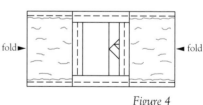

Figure 4

strips in place at the top and bottom edges, overlapping the facings.
9. Machine stitch through all thicknesses along both top and bottom edges, taking a ¼"-½" seam. Turn the cover right side out and press the narrow facing strips toward the batting at the seams. You may wish to fuse the facing strips in place with fusible web. Fit cover onto album by bending the album leaves back and sliding them into the sleeves of the fabric cover.

Twenty-Four-Block Sampler Quilt

BASKET
SAMPLERS

TWENTY-FOUR-BLOCK SAMPLER QUILT

Finished size: 53½" x 69½"
Twenty-four 6" Basket Blocks

The sampler shown in the photograph on page 94 features 6" basket blocks. Starting at the top left, the baskets included are: Row 1: Tiny Baskets, Valentine Basket, Grape Basket and Bow-Knot Basket. Row 2: Simple Basket, Cactus Basket, Bread Basket and Fruit Basket. Row 3: State Fair Basket, Cherry Basket, Cake Stand and Springtime Basket. Row 4: Dresden Basket, A May Basket, Parquet Basket and Diamond Tulip Basket. Row 5: Flowerpot Basket, New York Basket, Cathy's Tulip Basket and Basket of Flowers. Row 6: Kitten Basket, Bunny Basket, Garden Basket and Orange Basket.

YARDAGES

2½ yards Fabric #1 (dark green print) for outer border, setting pieces, pieced border units and basket patchwork

2¼ yards Fabric #2 (light green print) for inner border, pieced border units and background of basket blocks

½ yard Fabric #3 (medium green print) for pieced border units and basket patchwork

½ yard Fabric #4 (cranberry solid) for narrow border and basket patchwork

½ yard Fabric #5 (floral print) for pieced border units and basket patchwork

Scraps or ⅛ yard each of 6-8 assorted pink, cranberry, and green fabrics for basket patchwork

4½ yards backing fabric

Batting, larger than 53½" x 69½"

CUTTING INSTRUCTIONS

Always cut borders and binding strips from yardage before cutting smaller pieces for patchwork. Measurements given for borders and binding are 2-3" longer than needed. Exact trimming will be done when the borders are sewn to the quilt top.

1. Make templates for pieced border unit Patterns V, W, X, Y and Z on page 98. Patterns are finished size; add ¼" seam allowances when cutting pieces from fabric.

2. From Fabric #1 (dark green), cut two 4½" x 74" border strips and two 4½" x 57" border strips for the outer border. Referring to the general instructions, page 17, cut 15 setting squares, 16 half-block triangles, and four quarter-block corner triangles. Using Template X, mark and cut 48 triangles for the pieced border units.

3. From Fabric #2 (light green), cut two 3½" x 44" border strips and two 3½" x 61" border strips for the inner border. Using Template W, mark and cut 96 triangles for the pieced border units. Using Templates Y and Z, cut four Y rectangles and four Z rectangles.

4. From Fabric #3 (medium green), use Template X to mark and cut 48 triangles for the pieced border units.

5. From Fabric #4 (cranberry), cut six 1¼" wide strips across the fabric width for the narrow border.

6. From Fabric #5 (floral print), use Template V to mark and cut 52 squares for the pieced border units and corners.

7. From the assorted scrap fabrics and the remaining fabrics, cut pieces for twenty-four 6" baskets of your choice.

SEWING INSTRUCTIONS

1. Piece twenty-four 6" basket blocks. Refer to the general instructions for tips on patchwork, appliqué and basket handles.

2. Set the blocks together with the setting blocks, half-block triangles and quarter-block corner triangles as shown in the diagram. The inner quilt should measure approximately 34½" x 51½", including seam allowances.

3. Sew the Fabric #2 (light green) borders to the quilt top.

4. To piece one border unit, refer to Figure 1 and sew a W triangle to two adjacent sides of a V square, forming a triangle. Sew a Fabric #1 (dark green) X triangle to the left side of the pieced triangle and a Fabric #2 (medium green) triangle to the right side. Make a total of 48 border units.

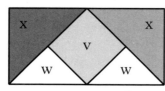

Pieced Border Unit

Figure 1

5. To make the top and bottom pieced borders, sew together 10 pieced units for each border. Sew the pieced borders to the top and bottom of the quilt top.

6. Sew together 14 pieced units for each side border. To make a pieced border corner, refer to Figure 2. Sew a light green Y rectangle to one side of a V floral square; add a Z rectangle along the adjacent side, forming a square. Make four border corners. Sew a border corner unit onto the ends of the side borders. Sew the side borders to the quilt top, stretching the pieced borders slightly to fit the quilt top.

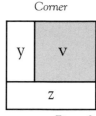

Pieced Border Corner

Figure 2

7. To make the narrow borders for the top and bottom, sew together three Fabric #4 strips into one long strip. Cut the strip in half, making two borders. To make the borders for the sides, sew pairs of Fabric #4 strips together. Sew borders to the quilt top.

8. Sew the Fabric #1 borders to the quilt top, mitering border corner seams.

9. Quilt as desired and bind outer edges.

Pieced Border Pattern
for Twenty-Four-Block
Sampler Quilt

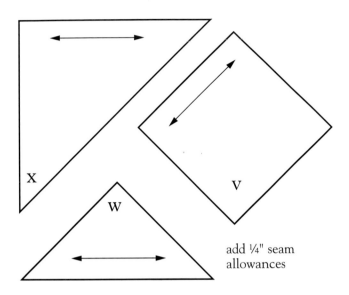

x

v

w

add ¼" seam
allowances

Pieced Border Corner Pattern
for Twenty-Four-Block
Sampler Quilt

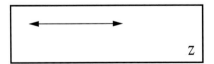

z

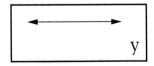

y

add ¼" seam allowances

NINE-BLOCK SAMPLER WALL QUILT

Finished size: 31½" x 31½"
Nine 6" Basket Blocks

The sampler shown in the photograph on page 99 features 6" basket blocks. Starting at the top left, the baskets included are: Row 1: A May Basket, Cake Stand, Cherry Basket. Row 2: Diamond Tulip Basket, Cathy's Tulip Basket, and State Fair Basket. Row 3: Springtime Basket, Cactus Basket, and Parquet Basket.

YARDAGE

1 yard Fabric #1 (blue print) for outer border, setting pieces, and basket patchwork
½ yard Fabric #2 (cream) for background of basket blocks
½ yard Fabric #3 (pink print) for inner border and basket patchwork
⅜ yard Fabric #4 (blue) for binding
Scraps or ⅛ yard each of approximately 6-8 different pink and blue fabrics for basket patchwork
1 yard backing fabric
Batting, larger than 31½"x 31½"

CUTTING INSTRUCTIONS

Always cut borders and binding strips from yardage before cutting smaller pieces for patchwork. Measurements given for borders and binding are 2-3" longer than needed. Exact trimming will be done when the borders are sewn to the quilt top.

1. From Fabric #1 (blue print), cut four 2½" x 36" strips for outer border. Cut four setting squares, eight half-block setting triangles, and four quarter-block corner triangles. Refer to the general instructions, page 17, for instructions for cutting setting pieces.

2. From Fabric #3 (pink print), cut four 1½" x 31" strips for inner border.

3. From Fabric #4 (blue), cut four 2½" wide binding strips across the fabric width.

4. From the remaining fabrics and the various scrap fabrics, cut pieces for nine 6" basket blocks of your choice.

SEWING INSTRUCTIONS

1. Piece nine 6" basket blocks. Refer to the general instructions for tips on patchwork, appliqué and basket handles.

2. Set the blocks together with the setting blocks, half-block triangles and quarter-block corner triangles as shown in the diagram right. The inner quilt should measure 26" x 26", including seam allowances.

3. Refer to the general instructions, page 18, on adding and mitering borders.

4. Quilt as desired. The setting pieces on the sampler below are quilted with the Cactus Basket motif. Use finished-size templates for the 6" Cactus Basket block to mark the quilting design.

5. After quilting, add binding as described in the general instructions.

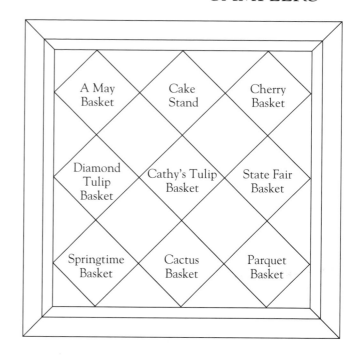

A May Basket · Cake Stand · Cherry Basket · Diamond Tulip Basket · Cathy's Tulip Basket · State Fair Basket · Springtime Basket · Cactus Basket · Parquet Basket

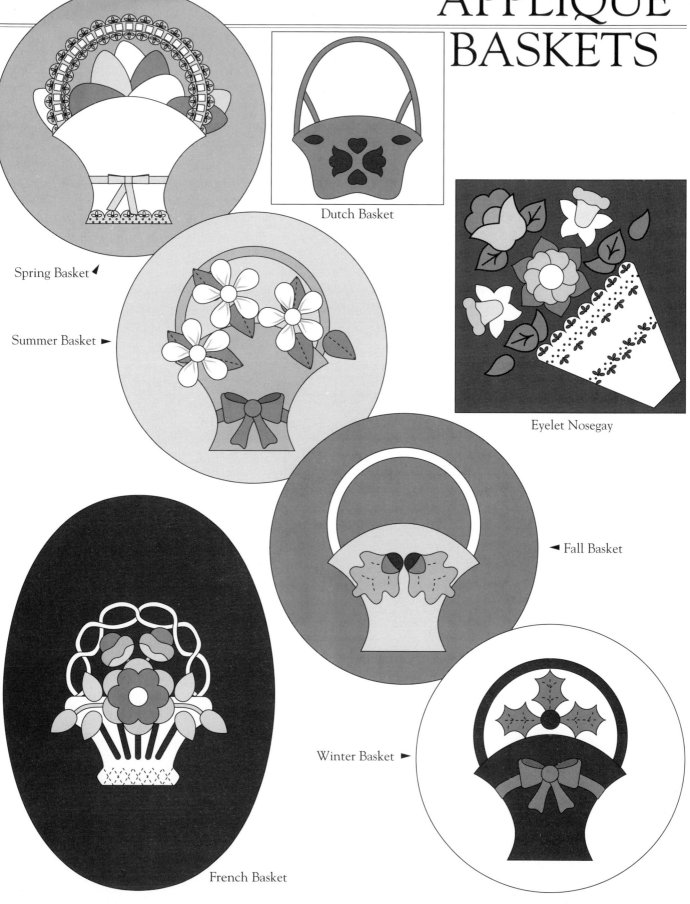

Spring Basket ◄

Summer Basket ►

Dutch Basket

Eyelet Nosegay

◄ Fall Basket

Winter Basket ►

French Basket

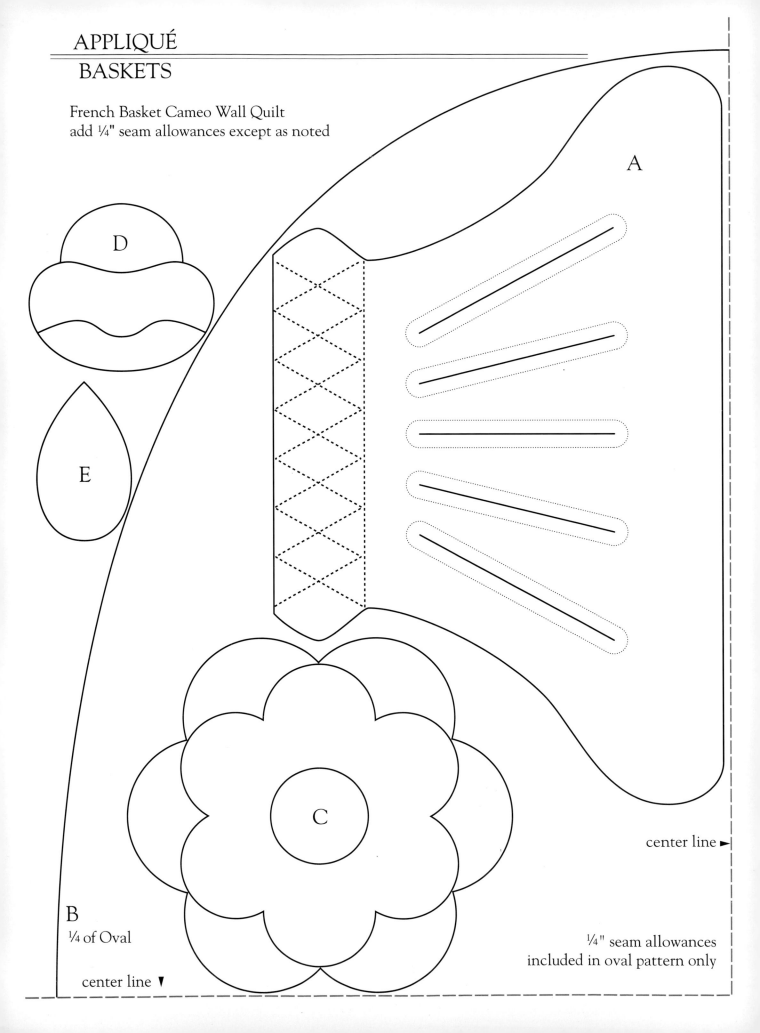

APPLIQUÉ
BASKETS

French Basket Cameo Wall Quilt
add ¼" seam allowances except as noted

A

D

E

C

B
¼ of Oval

center line ▼

center line ▶

¼" seam allowances
included in oval pattern only

Eyelet Nosegay Basket
add ¼" seam allowances

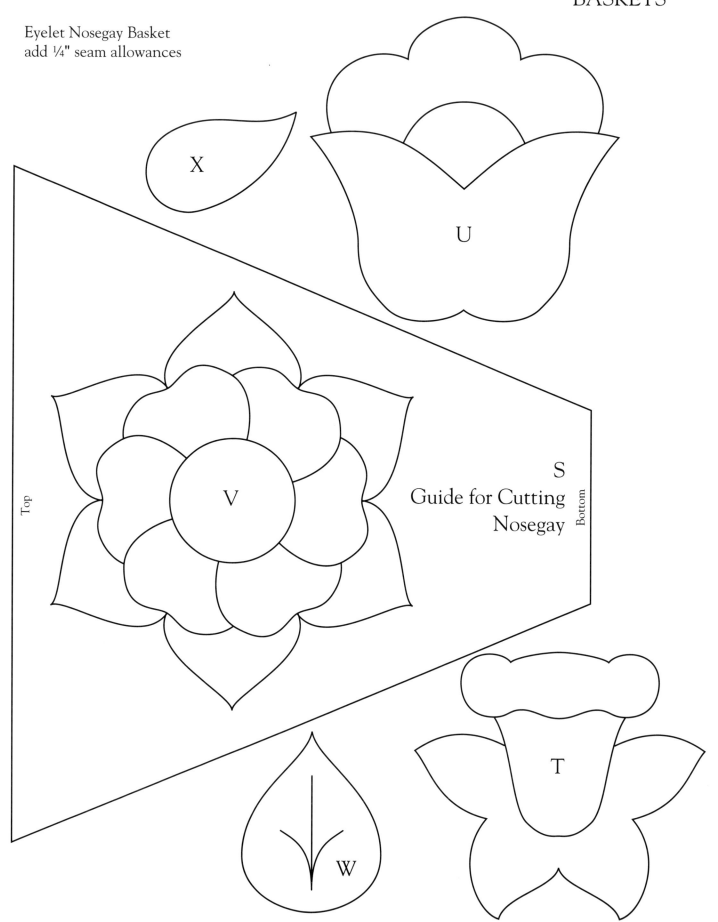

X

U

Top

V

S
Guide for Cutting
Nosegay

Bottom

W

T

APPLIQUÉ
BASKETS

Dutch Basket and Appliqués
add ¼" seam allowances

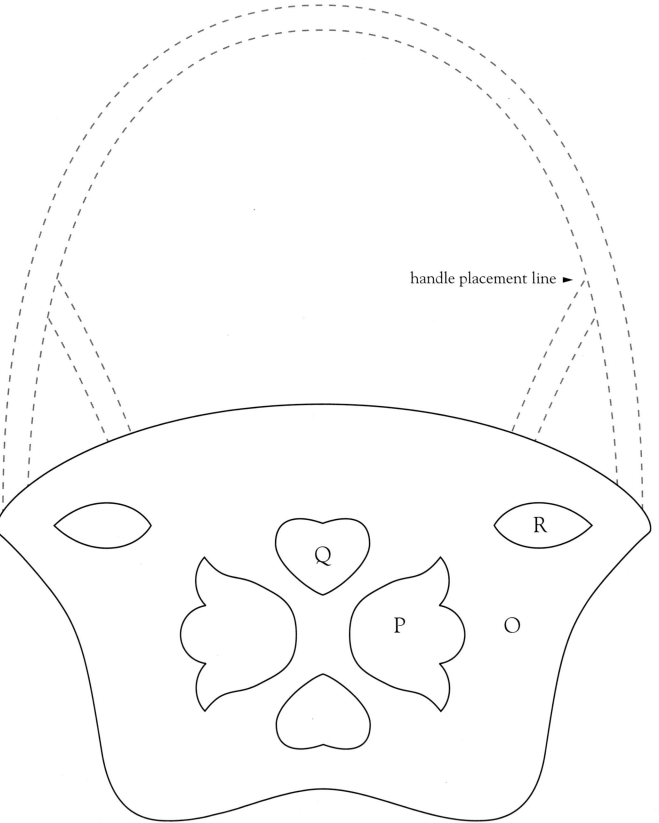

handle placement line ►

APPLIQUÉ
BASKETS
Season Baskets
add ¼" seam allowances
(except as noted)

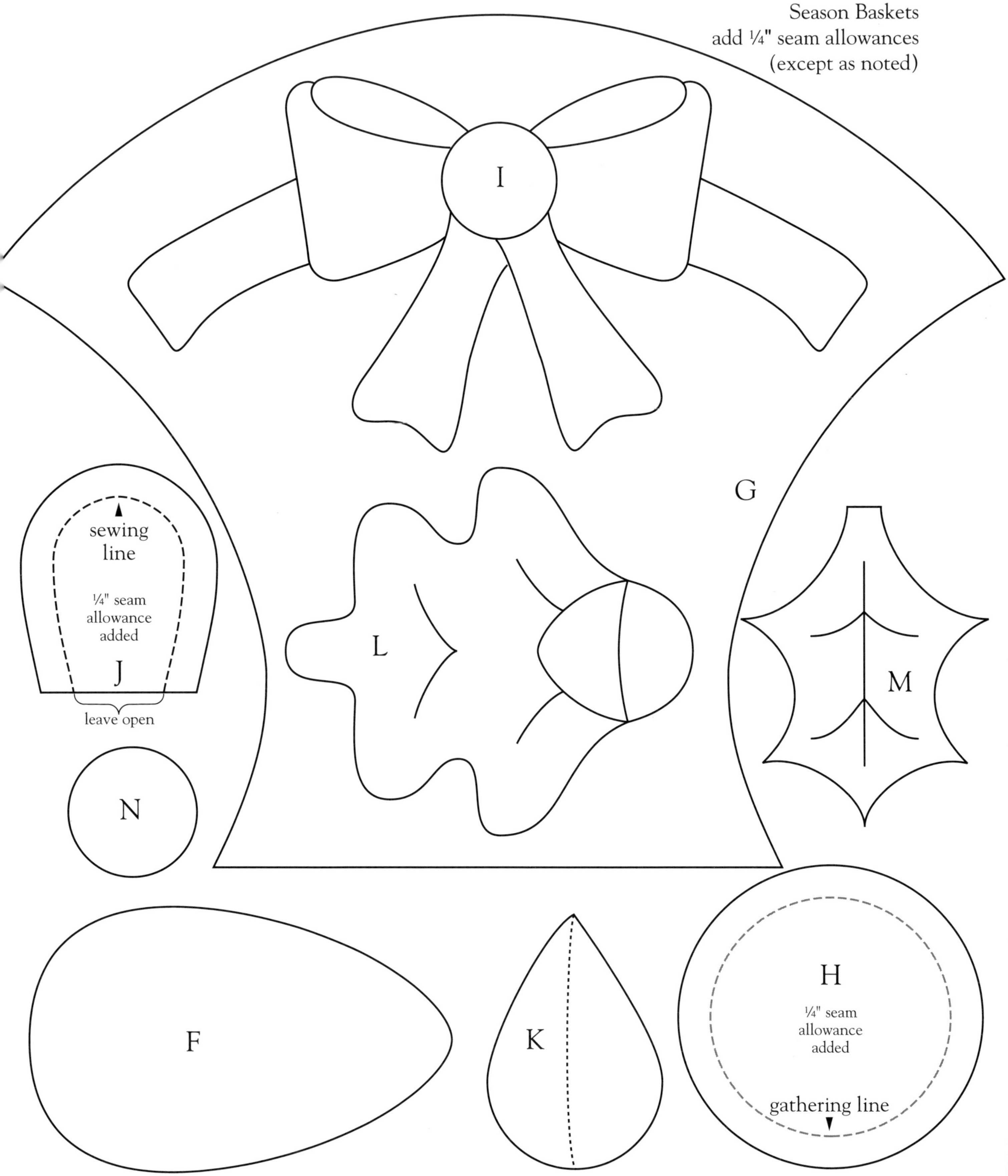

I

G

sewing
line

¼" seam
allowance
added

J

leave open

L

M

N

F

K

H

¼" seam
allowance
added

gathering line

FRENCH BASKET CAMEO WALL QUILT

Finished Size: 36" x 42"
French Basket Block

The quilt shown below features the French Basket block. Instructions are given for that block, but any appliquéd basket which will fit on the oval background can be used.

YARDAGE

2 yards Fabric #1 (dark green) for cameo oval, outer border and binding

¾ yard Fabric #2 (medium green print) for inner rectangle and leaves

½ yard Fabric #3 (dusty rose solid) for narrow inner border, piping around oval, flowers and buds

½ yard Fabric #4 (green micro-dot) for meandering vine on outer border

¼ yard Fabric #5 (beige solid) for French Basket and handle

Various scraps of eight or more dark, medium and light rose prints for flowers and buds

1¾ yards of ⅛" wide cotton cording for piping

1⅜ yards each of backing fabric and batting

CUTTING INSTRUCTIONS

1. From Fabric #1, cut (on crosswise grain) two border strips 8" x 45" and two border strips 8" x 39". The borders are cut 2"-3" longer than needed – exact trimming will be done when they are sewn onto the quilt top and mitered. Also on the crosswise grain, cut four binding strips 2½" x 45" and a 16" x 24" rectangle for the center oval.

2. From Fabric #2, cut a background rectangle 20½" x 26½". From the remainder, cut 90 leaves (6 for the center and 84 for border vine). Patterns for the appliqués are on page 102.

3. From Fabric #3, cut two border strips 1" x 24" and two borders 1" x 30", cutting on the crosswise grain. Cut five flowers (one for the center and for each corner). Cut a 10" square from which you can make 1" wide continuous bias to encase the cording for piping. Use the remainder of this fabric for some of the appliqué buds.

4. Cut an 18" square from Fabric #4 to make 1" wide continuous bias for the meandering vine and stems.

5. Using the pattern on page 102, cut one French Basket from Fabric #5. Use remaining fabric for the handle.

6. From the remaining fabrics, cut appliqué pieces to make a total of 30 buds and 5 flowers; you will use Patterns E, D and C. (Cut green for the bottom section of Pattern D for only the two center buds.)

QUILT INSTRUCTIONS

1. Center the basket, handle and contents on the rectangle for the center oval. Refer to the general instructions for tips on appliqué and handles. For the reverse appliqué on the basket, slit the basket fabric on the indicated lines (see Pattern A, page 102). Turn under the edges of each slit and appliqué them in place, exposing the background fabric.

2. Use Pattern B on page 102 to make a ¼-oval template. Fold the center rectangle fabric in quarters and place the template with the curved edge on the outside of the folded fabric. Cut away the outer edges of the rectangle. Our oval pattern includes seam allowances, so it is not necessary to add them before cutting. When the oval is cut, baste under the ¼" seam allowance around the outer edge of the oval.

3. Make piping by encasing the cotton cording in the Fabric #3 bias. Fold the bias in half, placing the cording in the fold. Use a zipper foot or a piping foot to machine stitch close to the cording.

4. Appliqué the oval onto the inner rectangle, with the piping placed between the layers so it is sewn in place with the appliqué. Where ends of piping meet, clip away the cording on one end and fold in the raw edge of the bias. Slip remaining piping end into the fold.

5. Sew on the narrow border and wide outer border. Refer to the general instructions on mitering borders (page 18).

6. Press the bias for the vine into thirds, making sure the underneath raw edge is covered by a top fold. Baste vine in place on outer border, keeping opposite borders as symmetrical as possible.

7. Position leaves, buds and corner flowers along the vine as desired. Appliqué each piece in place.

8. To finish the quilt, refer to the general instructions on quilting and binding.

GARDEN MAZE BABY QUILT

Finished Size: 39" x 51"
9" Dutch Basket Block

The quilt shown on page 100 features the Dutch Basket used as a 9" block. If you wish to substitute an Upright Basket in the setting as diagrammed, you will need to draft your own patterns for a 9" basket block.

Dutch Basket design is by Dorothy Crowdes.

YARDAGE

1 yard Fabric #1 (navy micro-dot) for sashing, set squares and binding
1¾ yards Fabric #2 (muslin) for background squares, sashing and set squares

(continued on page 108)

APPLIQUÉ
BASKETS

¼ yard burgundy solid for appliqués
18" x 22" each of six assorted indigo prints for baskets and basket handles
1½ yards backing fabric
1½ yards batting

CUTTING INSTRUCTIONS

1. From Fabric #1, cut four strips for binding, 2½" x 45", and one strip 2½" x 18", cutting on the crosswise grain. Cut 16 crosswise strips for the garden maze setting, each 1" x 40".

2. From Fabric #2, cut eight sashing strips 2½" x 40", cutting on the crosswise grain. For the Dutch Basket, cut 12 basket background squares, each 9½" square.

3. Patterns a, b and c for the setting squares are given below. Make templates for each of the three shapes. From Fabric #1, cut 20 of Pattern a and 36 of Pattern c. Cut 72 of Triangle b from Fabric #2. Or, to quick cut the b triangles, cut eighteen 3¼" squares. Divide each square diagonally both ways to produce four triangles per square.

4. From the remaining fabrics, cut the appropriate pieces to make 12 basket blocks of your choice. For the Dutch Basket, cut two baskets and handles from each of the six prints. Patterns for the Dutch Basket are on page 104.

QUILT INSTRUCTIONS

1. Make 12 basket blocks. Refer to the general instructions on making curved handles and tips on appliqué.

2. Make 16 setting squares using Patterns a, b and c as shown below. Make four more units for the corners, which are partial squares that end with the central diagonal bar (a) as shown in the diagram on page 107.

3. Sew one Fabric #1 sashing strip to either side of each Fabric #2 sashing strip to make eight units as shown below, each 40" long. Then, cut each strip combination into 9½" lengths. You need 31 sashing units to make the quilt as diagrammed.

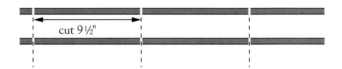

cut 9½"

4. Referring to the diagram, combine sashing units with basket blocks to construct three vertical rows. Combine the remaining sashing strips with the setting squares, constructing four vertical rows as shown, with the appropriate corner squares at either end of two of these rows.

5. Matching corners and seams carefully, sew rows together to complete the quilt top.

6. To finish the quilt, refer to the general instructions on quilting and binding.

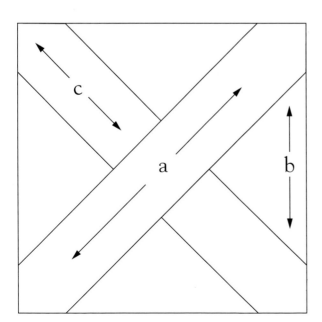

PLAID BASKETS
Four Seasons Hoop Wallhangings

Finished Size: 14" Diameter
Spring, Summer, Fall & Winter Basket Blocks

The four wallhangings shown on page 110 feature each of the Four Season blocks. Instructions are given for each of these blocks, but any appliquéd block which will fit inside the hoop can be used.

YARDAGE/SUPPLIES

(for each basket, as shown on page 110)
18" square of background fabric
¼ yard plaid for basket and handle, if desired
Scraps for basket trim, fillers and handle, if desired
18" square each of backing fabric and batting
1⅝ yard of 2½"-3" wide bias for hoop casing (or make
    3" wide bias from a 15" fabric square
14" quilting hoop

Additional notions for Spring Basket:
¾ yard of ⅝" wide satin ribbon for bow
½ yard of ¼" wide satin ribbon for handle
½ yard double ruffle eyelet beading for handle
6" of 1" wide flat eyelet lace for bottom trim

INSTRUCTIONS

1. Patterns for the basket and contents are on page 105. Cut appliqués as desired, using the appropriate patterns. Use Pattern G to cut the basket(s) from plaid fabric on the bias.

2. Appliqué the basket(s) and contents to background fabric as desired. The Spring Basket bow is made by appliquéing a strip of ribbon across the basket 3" up from the base. Tie the remaining ribbon in a bow and tack it in place. Refer to the general instructions for tips on appliqué.

Steps 3-5 apply to Summer Basket only

3. Cut 10 petals and one center for each dimensional daisy. Sew two petals right sides together with a ¼" seam, leaving end open to turn. Clip and trim seam allowances. Turn petals to right side out and press.

4. Fold the petal centers in thirds to make a pleat. Tack five pleated petals to the background fabric for each daisy.

5. Run a gathering thread ¼" from the outer edge of each daisy center. Draw the circle up tight, inserting a small bit of polyester filling. Appliqué the centers over the daisy petals.

6. Assemble the appliquéd basket(s) with batting and backing fabric and fit all three layers into the quilt hoop. Quilt as desired. (Refer to the general instructions for tips on quilting.)

FINISHING THE HOOP

1. Center the project carefully in the hoop. Mark the background fabric along the back edge of the hoop as shown at right. Remove the work from the hoop.

2. Press the wide prepared bias strip in half lengthwise, making it 1½" wide. Lay the raw edges of the bias on the drawn line of the background fabric. The folded edge of the bias is toward the inside of the circle.

3. Machine stitch the bias to the background fabric through all layers, ¼" from the raw edge of the bias. Before stitching, tuck the beginning end of the bias inside the casing. Be sure the casing opening corresponds with the top of the basket. Tuck in the finishing end of bias as you complete the stitching of the circle.

4. Trim excess background fabric, batting and backing even with the raw edge of the casing. Turn the casing to the back of the piece. Insert a cord or string in the casing. Position the work over the inner ring of the hoop; draw the cord tight and tie. Fit the outer hoop on and tighten it. Retie string if necessary to take up slack.

EYELET NOSEGAY PILLOW

Finished Size: 18¾" x 18¾" (including ruffles)
Eyelet Nosegay Block

The yardage and instructions are for using the Eyelet Nosegay Block in a pillow, as shown at left, but any 12" block can be used for the pillow.

YARDAGE

¾ yard Fabric #1 (blue print) for outer ruffle, pillow back
⅜ yard Fabric #2 (blue print) for background square
¼ yard Fabric #3 (rose print) for inner ruffle, star flower
¼ yard of 6" wide flat eyelet lace for nosegay
2½ yards of 2½" wide ungathered eyelet for inner ruffle
⅛ yard or assorted scraps for flowers and leaves
Polyester filling for pillow stuffing

CUTTING INSTRUCTIONS

1. From Fabric #1, cut two ruffle strips 5" x 45". From the remainder, cut a 12½" square for the pillow back.
2. Cut a 12½" square from Fabric #2 for background.
3. From Fabric #3, cut two strips 3" x 45" for inner ruffle.

4. From remaining fabrics, cut flowers and leaves. Use the patterns given on page 103 or substitute other flowers.

PILLOW INSTRUCTIONS

1. Cut the wide eyelet as shown in Figure 1, using the cutting guide on page 103. Add seam allowances if you are making the pillow with hand appliqué. Using either hand or machine appliqué, sew the nosegay flowers and leaves onto the background square as desired. For tips on hand appliqué, see the general instructions.

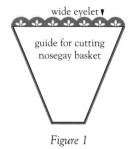

wide eyelet ▼

guide for cutting nosegay basket

Figure 1

2. Seam the two pieces of the outer ruffle fabric end to end to make a single strip 5" x 89½". Do the same for the inner ruffle fabric.

3. Match raw edges and right sides of the ruffle strips along one length and sew, taking a ¼" seam. Press the joined strips open to make a single strip, 7½" x 89½".

4. Bring the ends of the ruffle strip together and make a ¼" seam, creating a big loop. Press the ruffle loop in half lengthwise, wrong sides together. Sew the eyelet lace into a loop and place it around the ruffle loop with the wrong side of the eyelet against the right side of the inner ruffle, matching raw edges.

5. Mark off four equal sections on the ruffle fabric. Run two lines of large gathering stitches ¼" from the raw edge of the ruffle loop.

6. Mark the midpoint of each side of the pillow top with a pin. Match and pin the quarter division marks of the ruffle loop to the middle of each side of the pillow square with the eyelet against the right side of the pillow and raw edges together.

7. Draw up the gathering thread on the ruffle, spacing the gathers evenly along the pillow edge and allowing lots of extra fullness at the corners. Rounding off the corners slightly when positioning the ruffle will keep the stuffed pillow from looking "dog-eared." Machine baste the gathered ruffle to the pillow top with a ¼" seam allowance. To keep the ruffle from being caught in the seam when the back is sewn on, "baste" the ruffle to the pillow top with bits of masking tape.

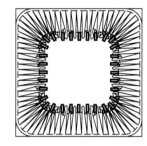

Figure 2

8. Pin the pillow back to the front, right sides together. The ruffle is hidden between top and back. Machine stitch around the pillow, taking a ⅜" seam allowance. Leave a 6" opening in one side for turning and stuffing. To ensure the gathering stitches are hidden, sew this seam with the pillow top side up.

9. Turn the pillow right side out through the opening. Remove the masking tape. Stuff the pillow firmly with polyester filling. Slip stitch the opening closed.

Baskets, Big and Little

Illinois quilter Marian Brockschmidt started her Baltimore-style basket block in a workshop. Marian liked her work so well, she let it grow into a full-size quilt, using six-inch pieced basket blocks to complement the appliqué center block. The basket shape is on pages 116-117. A detail photo of the center block is included on page 115.

WOVEN APPLIQUÉ BASKETS

Red Flower Basket

Lattice Basket

Bowl of Flowers

Baltimore Basket

Trellis Basket

GENERAL INSTRUCTIONS

The beautiful Baltimore Album quilts of the mid-nineteenth century are generously sprinkled with baskets and urns made from narrow strips of fabric interwoven and appliquéd on background fabric. Crewel embroidered spreads of an earlier period exhibit basket motifs with interwoven grids of embroidery thread that duplicate the look of a basket's woven fibers.

The woven appliqué basket projects presented on these pages are all inspired by antique quilts. They grew out of our general interest in basket designs and a natural curiosity about how these old-time quilt baskets were formed. We discovered that even elaborate basket designs work up rapidly. These woven baskets make lovely focal points for special projects.

We hope that you will study the instructions for this technique and then experiment with basket shape ideas of your own.

PLANNING THE BASKET SHAPE

Make a template of the basket outline and trace the shape onto your background fabric. Outline shapes for each project are provided.

You can add extra interest to the basket by using a fabric underlay cut slightly smaller than the basket outline. Position the fabric underlay on the background fabric within the basket outline. The fabric strips will be woven over the underlay, and the underlay, instead of the background fabric, will show through the weaving.

If you wish to design your own basket, begin with a full-size outline sketch and make a template to use as described above. Folding and cutting paper into a basket shape is an easy way to create a symmetrical basket outline. An alternate method is to design the basket directly on the background (or underlay) fabric. Use narrow strips of masking tape the width of the fabric strips you intend to use. Stick the tape lightly to the fabric, positioning and repositioning the tape until you achieve a strip arrangement and basket shape you like. Mark along the edges of the tape strips onto the fabric with a removable marker. Lift the tape off and use the marks as guides in placing the fabric strips.

CHOOSING FABRIC FOR STRIPS:

Weaving strips may be cut all of one fabric or several different fabrics. Striped fabrics, cut with the stripe, make interesting weavings. (See Lattice Basket pictured on page 125.) Strip width should be kept in scale to the basket and total project. Generally, a finished strip width of ¼" to 1" works well. Strip widths in a project may be kept uniform as in the Trellis Basket or varied for extra interest as in the Baltimore Basket (page 122).

Strips cut on the straight of grain of the fabric work best for most weaving because they will not stretch. Only strips that must curve should be bias strips. Try to avoid having seams in the weaving pieces. If you must use bias, cut individual strips of the needed length rather than making continuous bias. Refer to the general instructions on cutting individual bias strips such as for basket handles.

PREPARING FABRIC STRIPS FOR WEAVING

Cut long narrow strips of fabric just less than three times the finished width. For example, cut strips ⅝"-¾" for a finished width of about ¼". Remember, strips should be cut on the straight of grain unless they need to curve in the design.

Fold the strips in thirds along their length and press well as you go, keeping the bottom raw edge hidden beneath the fold. Bias strips for curves will be easier to handle if they are basted after pressing.

WEAVING AND APPLIQUÉING THE BASKET

Position the prepared fabric strips on the basket outline. Cut the strips to length as you lay out and weave the strips. A fabric glue stick, used sparingly, is a convenient way to hold the strips in place as you weave. Add thread basting as needed to secure strips for appliqué.

Flower and leaf patterns are given for the projects shown. Plan your own flower arrangement by using other flowers from this book or designing your own.

Appliqué basket contents and handle and then along both sides of the woven strips. Remember to appliqué the inner edge, then the outer edge of handles and other curves to keep curves smooth. For more tips on appliqué technique, refer to the general instructions.

WOVEN APPLIQUÉ GARMENTS

Woven appliqué baskets make excellent embellishments for garments, whether for the front of a dress or jumper, or the back of a vest or jacket. When choosing a garment pattern for a woven applique garment, pick one with an area big enough to accommodate a basket motif attractively.

Once you've selected a garment pattern, use it to cut out the fabric piece that will have the basket embellishment. Work with the garment piece just as you would a background block. Design your basket and flowers as described above in the general instructions.

For dresses and jumpers, you may wish to line the garment piece to protect and reinforce it and forego quilting.

Detail of center block of Marian Brockschmidt's Baltimore-Style Basket Quilt. See page 112 for a photo of the entire quilt.

WOVEN APPLIQUÉ
BASKETS
Baltimore Basket and Basket Appliqués – add ¼" seam allowances
except to basket shape

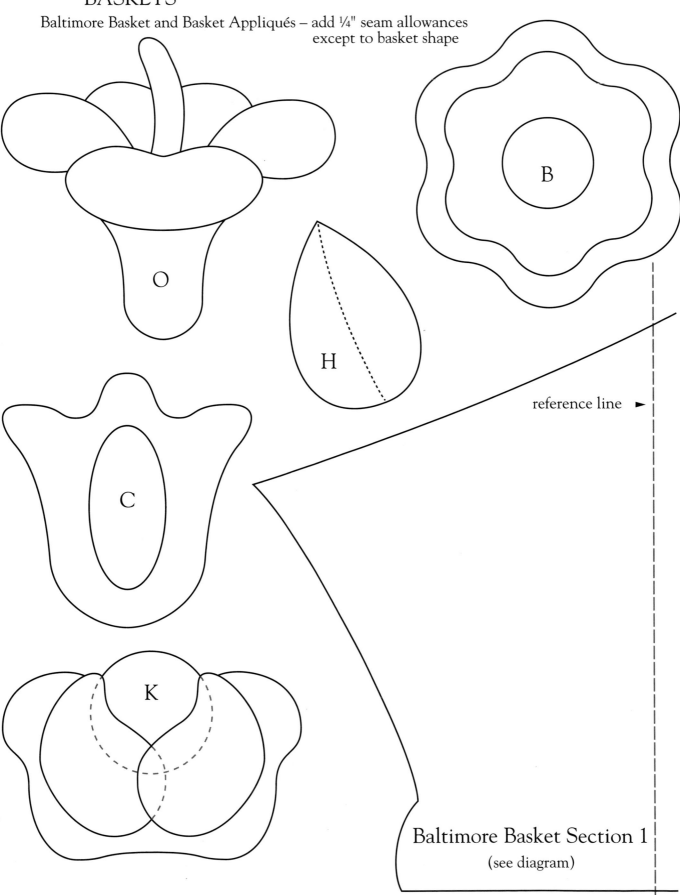

O

B

H

reference line ►

C

K

Baltimore Basket Section 1

(see diagram)

Baltimore Basket and Basket Appliqués (continued)
add ¼" seam allowances except to basket shape

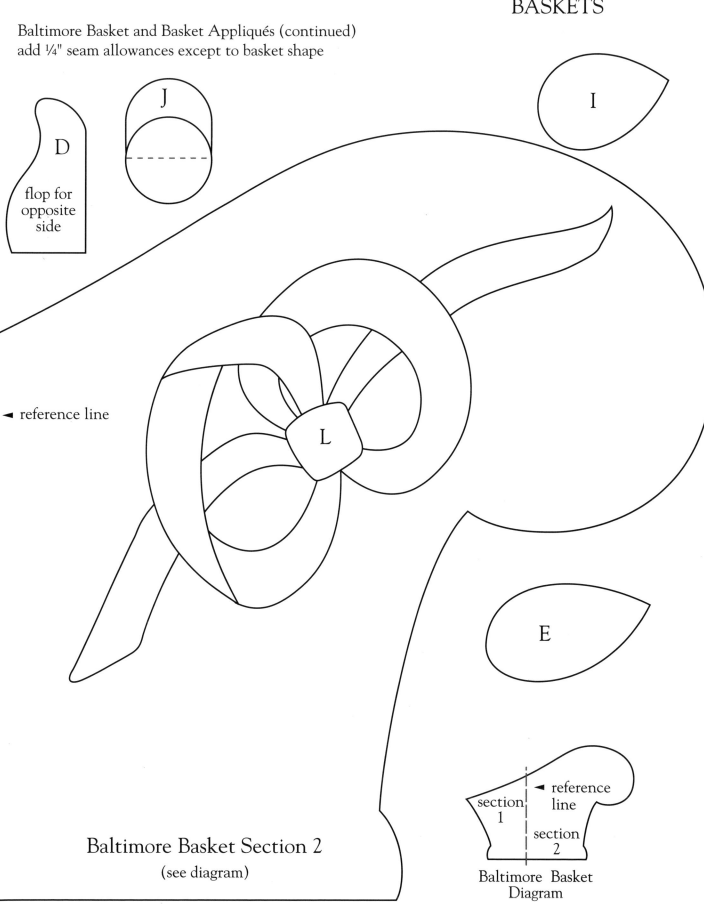

J

D

flop for
opposite
side

I

◄ reference line

L

E

Baltimore Basket Section 2

(see diagram)

section
1

◄ reference
line

section
2

Baltimore Basket
Diagram

Trellis Basket
add ¼" seam allowances
except to basket shape

Basket Template

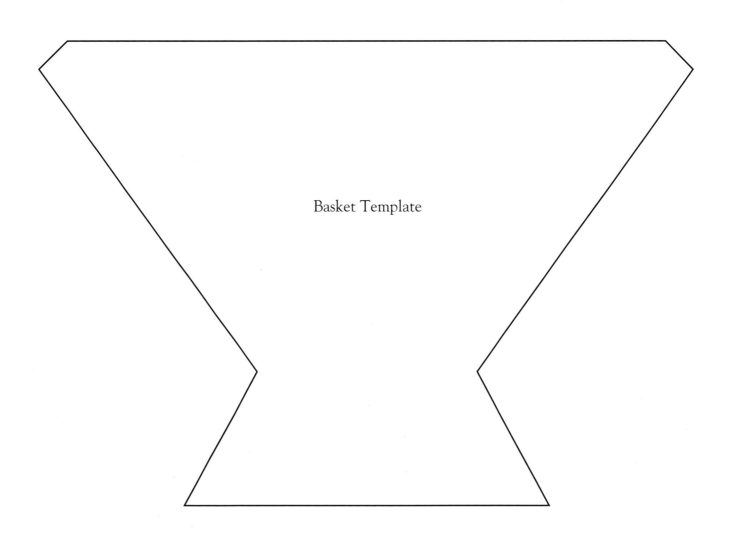

Basket Template

Bowl of
Flowers Basket

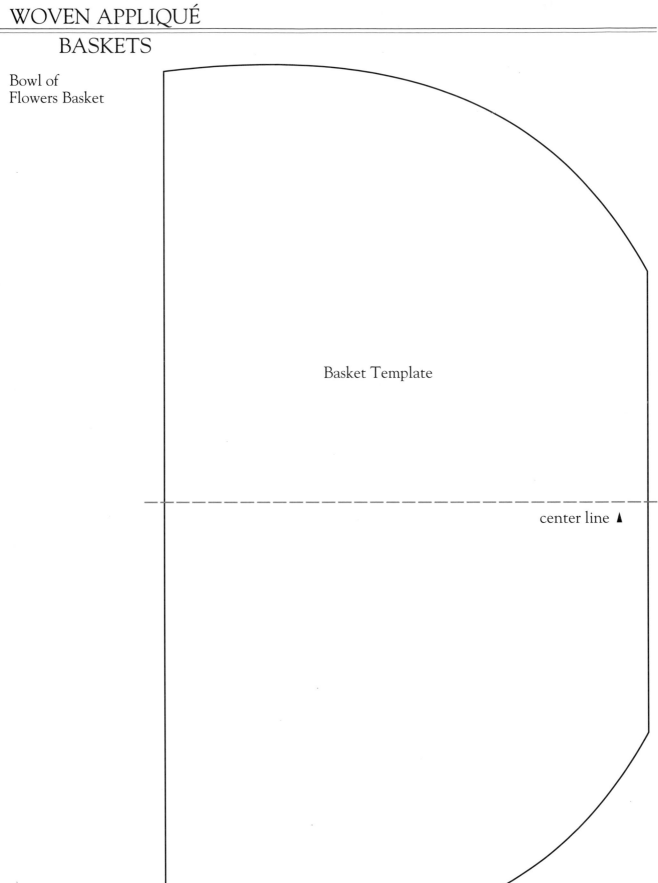

Basket Template

center line ▲

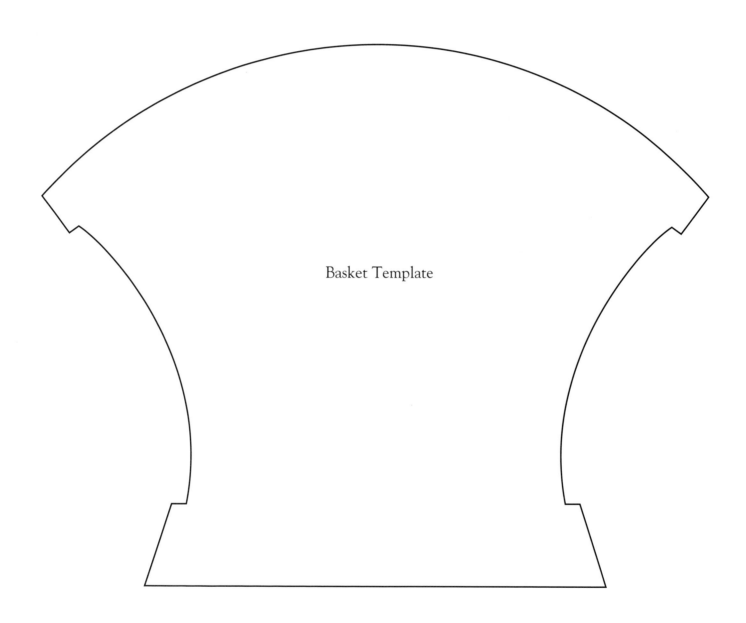

Basket Template

BALTIMORE BASKET WALL QUILT

Finished Size: 34" x 36"
17" Baltimore Basket Block

This simplified Baltimore-style basket is appliquéd to a rectangular center panel that finishes 22" x 24". You may substitute another basket shape in this setting or design a basket of your own. Lots of quilting and an interwoven bias outer border add interest to the center basket.

YARDAGE

1½ yards Fabric #1 (muslin) for background and outer borders

1¼ yards Fabric #2 (red solid) for weaving strips, basket handle, inner border and binding

½ yard each of two fabrics (solid blue and purple) for woven bias borders

Various scraps for appliquéd flowers, leaves, buds, bow and butterfly

1 yard each of backing fabric and batting

CUTTING INSTRUCTIONS

1. From Fabric #1 (muslin), cut two border strips 6" x 40" and two border strips 6" x 38". Cut the border strips on the crosswise grain. These measurements are 2-3" longer than exact length needed. Exact trimming is done when borders are sewn to quilt top. Cut a background rectangle 22½" x 24½".

2. Cut four binding strips from Fabric #2 (red) on the crosswise grain, each 2½" x 45". Cut two inner border strips on the crosswise grain 1" x 27" and two strips 1" x 25". For weaving, cut four strips 1" x 28" for the vertical slats of the basket, one strip 1¼" x 28" for the horizontal slats and one strip 1½" x 7¼" for the basket base. These strips can be cut on either crosswise or lengthwise grain. From the remainder of this fabric, cut two 1" wide bias strips, 15" long, for the top curved edge of the basket. For the basket handle, cut one bias strip 1¼" x 19".

3. From the appropriate fabrics, cut flowers, leaves, vines, a floating streamer bow, butterfly or other appliqués as desired. Patterns for the appliqués used are on pages 116 to 118. Or, if you like, design your own basket contents.

QUILT INSTRUCTIONS

1. Following the instructions for woven appliqué baskets, position and weave the Baltimore Basket onto the background fabric. (Basket pattern is on pages 116 and 117.) Appliqué basket and flowers onto background fabric. See general instructions on bias handles and appliqué technique.

2. Refer to general instructions on adding and mitering fabric borders. Add inner and outer borders as shown.

3. Starting with two 18" fabric squares, make 1¼" wide continuous bias from two border fabrics. Press bias strips in thirds. Position bias on outer border, weaving the two colors over and under around the quilt. To aid in placement of bias loops, fold and lightly crease borders in fourths. Be sure to appliqué the inner curves of the bias first, then the outer curves.

4. To finish the wall quilt, refer to the general instructions on quilting and binding.

BOWL OF FLOWERS BLOCK

Finished Size: 17" x 17"
17" Bowl of Flowers Block

Maxine Engstrom used a rounded bowl shape for a woven appliqué basket abundantly full of flowers and leaves, positioning it diagonally on a large (17" finished) square. She added a narrow border and squared off the block with light-colored corner pieces that would show off pretty quilting.

YARDAGE

⅔ yard background fabric if making a 17" block
½ yard fabric for weaving
Various scraps for underlay, flowers, leaves and butterfly

CUTTING INSTRUCTIONS

1. Cutting on the straight grain, cut 1⅛" wide strips for weaving. Finished strip width in the example is approximately ⅜". Using the basket shape given on page 120, cut a basket underlay. Cut a bias strip approximately 18" long for a bottom rim strip.
2. Cut appliqués from scraps. Design your own bouquet or select from flowers and leaves in this section.

INSTRUCTIONS

1. Following the instructions for woven appliqué baskets, position the strips on the underlay and baste in place. Position the underlay with strips on the background fabric. Add the prepared bottom rim strip. Appliqué strips in place.
2. Appliqué flowers and leaves as desired. Refer to the general instructions for tips on appliqué.
3. Finish your block as a wall quilt or pillow.

TRELLIS BASKET WALL QUILT

Finished Size: 33" x 33"
15" Trellis Basket Block

The 15" finished basket block for this quilt is enhanced by border stripe frames and an interesting woven-strip middle border. The simple flowerpot shape needs only a few flowers. Butterflies at the corner squares complement the single butterfly inside the block.

YARDAGE

1 yard or 150 running inches Fabric #1 (rust/gold stripe) for inner and outer borders (fabric must have one stripe that can be used at 1¾" finished width and another that can be used at a 3½" finished width)*

1¼ yards Fabric #2 (pale gold print) for weaving strips, basket handle, border squares and binding

¾ yard Fabric #3 (rust print) for background of woven middle border

½ yard Fabric #4 (muslin) for background of basket

Various scraps for basket underlay, flowers, leaves, bow and butterfly

1 yard each of backing fabric and batting

A note about using striped fabric for quilt borders: The number of repeats of a particular stripe varies from one fabric to another. If a stripe you wish to use as a border is not printed four times across the width of the fabric, you will need to buy extra length. A yardage requirement is given for border stripe in running inches. For the quilt shown, both inner and outer borders were stripes on the same fabric.

CUTTING INSTRUCTIONS

1. From Fabric #1 (stripe fabric), cut four inner border strips, 2¼" x 22". Cut four outer border strips 4" x 36". These measurements are 2"-3" longer than exact length needed. Exact trimming is done when borders are sewn to quilt top.

2. Cut four binding strips from Fabric #2 (gold print), each 2½" x 36". Cut four 4¼" border squares. Use the remainder of this fabric to cut weaving strips for the basket and border. Cut 20 strips across the width of the fabric, each 1" x 22".

3. From Fabric #3 (rust print), cut four middle border strips 4¼" x 19".

4. Cut a 15½" square for background of basket.

5. Cut a basket underlay from a fabric scrap. The pattern for the basket shape is given on page 119.

6. From appropriate fabric scraps, cut appliqué flowers, leaves, a triple bow knot and butterflies to create a unique, attractive bouquet. Or, design your own basket contents to appliqué.

QUILT INSTRUCTIONS

1. Following the general instructions for woven appliqué baskets, position and weave the Trellis Basket on the fabric underlay. Appliqué basket and flowers onto background fabric. See general instructions on bias handles and appliqué technique.

2. Add inner border. See general instructions on adding and mitering borders.

3. Make the middle border by weaving prepared strips on the border pieces.

4. Appliqué four butterflies to the gold border squares. Add a square to each end of two of the woven border strips. Sew the borders without corners onto opposite sides of the quilt top. Sew the remaining border strips (with corners) onto the remaining sides, matching seams at corners.

5. Add outer fabric border.

6. To finish the wall quilt, refer to general instructions on quilting and binding.

LATTICE BASKET BLOCK

Finished Size: 12" x 12"
Lattice Basket Block

The Lattice Basket shape works well for a rectangular block. The block in the photo is a narrow front panel for a dress, but the design could also be successful as a 12" block for a quilt or pillow.

YARDAGE

Fabric as needed for garment or background of block
¼ yard each of two fabrics for weaving
Various scraps for flowers and leaves of your choice

CUTTING INSTRUCTIONS

1. Cutting on the lengthwise grain, cut six to eight strips from each fabric. Finished strip width in the example shown is approximately ⅜"; the strips were cut 1⅛" wide. Strip width can vary (see instructions for woven appliqué baskets).
2. Cut appliqués from scraps. Design your own bouquet or select from flowers and leaves in this section.

INSTRUCTIONS

1. Following the instructions for woven appliqué baskets, position and weave the Lattice Basket on garment pattern piece or background fabric. The basket shape is on page 119. Appliqué strips in place.
2. Appliqué flowers and leaves as desired. Refer to the general instructions for tips on appliqué.
3. Complete your garment according to pattern instructions, or incorporate it into a quilt or pillow.

RED FLOWER BASKET

Finished Size: 12" to 15" Square

In this appliqué basket, the strips are not actually woven, just stitched to a darker underlay fabric. The block in the photo is on the front of an empire-waist jumper, but could also be used as a 12" to 15" block, depending on the arrangement of the flowers.

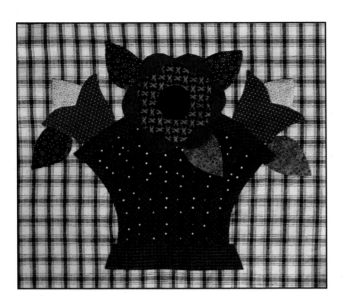

YARDAGE

Fabric as needed for garment or background of block
¼ yard of fabric for weaving
Various scraps for underlay, flowers and leaves

CUTTING INSTRUCTIONS

1. Use the Red Flower Basket shape on page 121 to cut an underlay if desired. Cut nine bias strips from the weaving fabric. Finished strip width in the example shown is a generous ¼"; the strips were cut 1" wide. Cut the bias strip for the basket rim 1⅜" wide to finish approximately ½" wide. For the basket base, cut a 1½" wide straight strip. Turn under ¼" seam allowances for the base, rather than folding in thirds.

2. Cut appliqué flowers and leaves from scraps. Design your own bouquet or select from flowers and leaves in this section.

INSTRUCTIONS

1. Following the instructions for woven appliqué baskets, position the strips on the underlay and baste in place. Position the underlay with strips on the pattern piece or background fabric. Add the prepared rim and base strips. Appliqué strips in place.

2. Appliqué flowers and leaves as desired. Refer to the general instructions for tips on appliqué.

3. Complete your garment according to pattern instructions, or incorporate it into a quilt or pillow.

Quilting Design for Sawtooth Border Wall Quilt
and other basket quilts

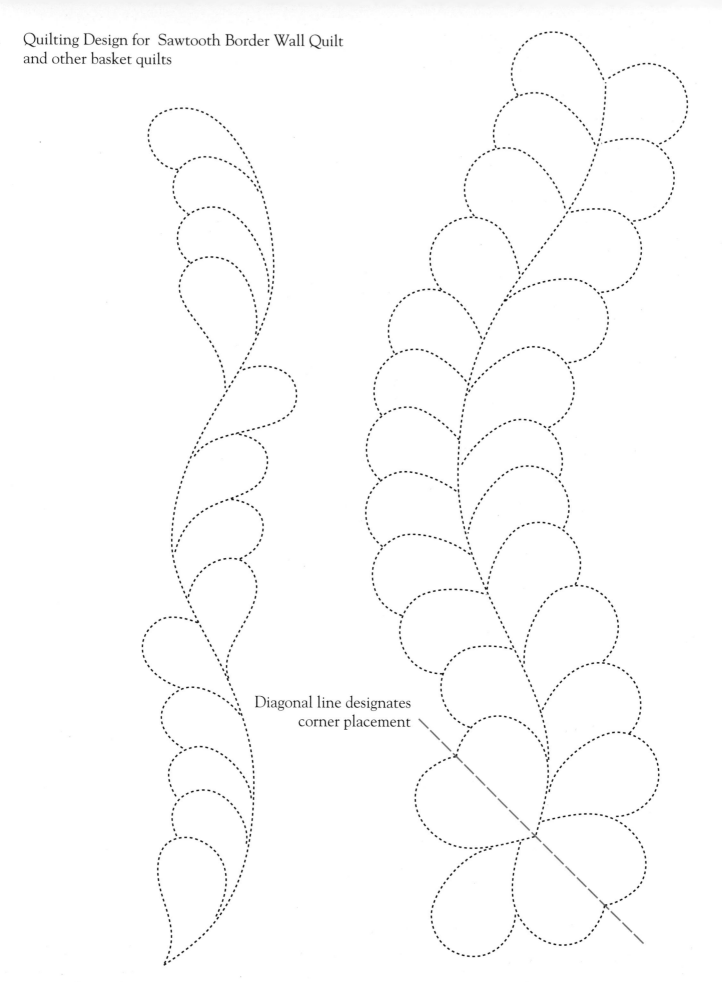

Diagonal line designates
corner placement

~ American Quilter's Society ~

dedicated to publishing books
for today's quilters

The following AQS publications are currently available:

American Beauties: Rose & Tulip Quilts
by Gwen Marston & Joe Cunningham
#1907: AQS, 1988, 96 pages, softbound, $14.95

America's Pictorial Quilts by Caron L. Mosey
#1662: AQS, 1985, 112 pages, hardbound, $19.95

Applique Designs: My Mother Taught Me to Sew
by Faye Anderson
#2121: AQS, 1990, 80 pages, softbound, $12.95

Arkansas Quilts: Arkansas Warmth
Arkansas Quilter's Guild, Inc.
#1908: AQS, 1987, 144 pages, hardbound, $24.95

The Art of Hand Applique, by Laura Lee Fritz
#2122: AQS, 1990, 80 pages, softbound, $14.95

...Ask Helen More About Quilting Designs by Helen Squire
#2099: AQS, 1990, 54 pages, 17 x 11, spiral-bound, $14.95

Classic Basket Quilts by Liz Porter and Marianne Fons
#2208: AQS, 1991, 128 pages, softbound, $16.95

A Collection of Favorite Quilts, by Judy Florence
#2119 AQS, 1990, 136 pages, softbound, $18.95

Dear Helen, Can You Tell Me?
...all about quilting designs by Helen Squire
#1820: AQS, 1987, 56 pages, 17 x 11, spiral-bound, $12.95

Dyeing & Overdyeing of Cotton Fabrics by Judy Mercer Tescher
#2030: AQS, 1990, 54 pages, softbound, $9.95

Fun & Fancy Machine Quiltmaking by Lois Smith
#1982: AQS, 1989, 144 pages, softbound, $19.95

Gallery of American Quilts: 1849-1988
#1938: AQS, 1988, 128 pages, softbound, $19.95

Gallery of American Quilts 1860-1989: Book II
#2129: AQS, 1990, 128 pages, softbound, $19.95

The Grand Finale: A Quilter's Guide to Finishing Projects
by Linda Denner
#1924: AQS, 1988, 96 pages, softbound, $14.95

Heirloom Miniatures by Tina M. Gravatt
#2097: AQS, 1990, 64 pages, softbound, $9.95

Home Study Course in Quiltmaking
by Jeannie M. Spears
#2031: AQS, 1990, 240 pages, softbound, $19.95

The Ins and Outs: Perfecting the Quilting Stitch
by Patricia J. Morris
#2120: AQS, 1990, 96 pages, softbound, $9.95

Irish Chain Quilts: A Workbook of Irish Chains & Related Patterns by Joyce B. Peaden
#1906: AQS, 1988, 96 pages, softbound, $14.95

Marbling Fabrics for Quilts: A Guide for Learning & Teaching
by Kathy Fawcett and Carol Shoaf
#2206: AQS, 1991, 72 pages, softbound, $12.95

Missouri Heritage Quilts by Bettina Havig
#1718: AQS, 1986, 104 pages, softbound, $14.95

Nancy Crow: Quilts and Influences by Nancy Crow
#1981: AQS, 1990, 256 pages, hardcover, $29.95

No Dragons on My Quilt by Jean Ray Laury with
Ritva Laury and Lizabeth Laury
#2153: AQS, 1990, 52 pages, hardcover, $12.95

Oklahoma Heritage Quilts Oklahoma Quilt Heritage Project
#2032: AQS, 1990, 144 pages, softbound, $19.95

Scarlet Ribbons: American Indian Technique for Today's Quilters by Helen Kelley
#1819: AQS, 1987, 104 pages, softbound, $15.95

Sets & Borders by Gwen Marston and Joe Cunningham
#1821: AQS, 1987, 104 pages, softbound, $14.95

Somewhere in Between: Quilts and Quilters of Illinois
by Rita Barrow Barber
#1790: AQS, 1986, 78 pages, softbound, $14.95

Stenciled Quilts for Christmas by Marie Monteith Sturmer
#2098: AQS, 1990, 104 pages, softbound, $14.95

Texas Quilts–Texas Treasures Texas Heritage Quilt Society
#1760: AQS, 1986, 160 pages, hardbound, $24.95

A Treasury of Quilting Designs, by Linda Goodmon Emery
#2029: AQS, 1990, 80 pages, 14 x 11, spiral-bound, $14.95

These books can be found in local bookstores and quilt shops. If you are unable to locate a title in your area, you can order by mail from AQS, P.O. Box 3290, Paducah, KY 42002-3290. Please add $1 for the first book and 40¢ for each additional one to cover postage and handling